Table of Conten

I0005182

Chapter 1 Introduction

Introducing Aurelia

Aurelia is a relatively new, open-source JavaScript library/framework that simplifies the creation of web-based applications. Building applications for the web is constantly changing, and new specifications are being introduced at an ever-increasing cadence. This calls for a framework that is forward-facing and embraces the new and upcoming technology landscape. Aurelia does this, and it does it very well. As we take a look at what it means to build an Aurelia application, you will be pleasantly surprised at how simple and easy it is to do things. This simplicity is hard to achieve, but architect Rob Eisenberg and his team have done exactly that. If you have been wanting to find a front-end framework that allows you to develop using ECMA-Script 2015 and ECMA-Script 2016, your wait is over. We will take a look at all the features of Aurelia and what makes it a serious contender for the front-end space when evaluating your next toolset.

History

Let's start with a little history. Rob Eisenberg has been famous for creating open-source frameworks for developers for a very long time. He started out by creating Caliburn, a framework for WPF and Silverlight developers. He then gave a talk on building your MVVM (model-view-viewmodel) framework that kick-started Caliburn.Micro, the second iteration of Caliburn. Next, he created Durandal, a front-end framework for JavaScript. It worked with Knockout and was very similar to Caliburn.Micro, but still very much an ES5 solution. Fast-forward to the beginning of 2015, and Rob announced Aurelia. This time, he decided to use features for the JavaScript language that were being introduced in ES6 and ES7, but were not yet ready. He was able to do this by transpiling the JavaScript code to an ES5-compliant version that current browsers could understand. *Transpilation* is the means of writing code in ES6 and ES7, and converting it to ES5 code. Transpilation does not compile your code, but simply changes it from one version of JavaScript to another. Microsoft's TypeScript is a good example of a superset of JavaScript that is transpiled to ES5 JavaScript. This is truly exciting, as it brings many new features to JavaScript that move the language closer to parity with mature languages such as Java and C#, but without the wait. You can code Aurelia applications using a lot of the same semantics and separation of concerns that you enjoy when developing in Java or C#.

Web components

One thing you will hear a lot is talk about web components. Most of the mature frameworks on the market today support this concept of allowing the developer to create components that encapsulate business logic and behavior for reuse in applications. Aurelia is no different, and it tries to adhere as closely as possible to the specification for web components. In Aurelia, they are called custom elements, so that any elements you create will work and play nicely with other frameworks, as well. Aurelia plays nicely with other frameworks and integrates easily with Polymer, for example.

Contents

Throughout the rest of the book, we will take a look at the core pieces that make up Aurelia. Aurelia was designed from the ground up to be modular. If there is a module that you don't want to use, or if you want to use another implementation, this is feasible, and the framework makes it very easy to do so. The first few chapters will be focused on getting your machine set up and going over the semantics of ES6 and ES7 features used throughout Aurelia. If you are not familiar with the syntax, don't worry—you will quickly become a fan.

Chapter 2 Getting Started

Getting set up

Sometimes the hardest part of learning a new framework is just getting started. It can be daunting when looking at all the ways to do things. Aurelia comes ready with a lot of implementations, and tries to allow developers to pick the route that best supports their programming paradigm. We will take a look at the options that are currently available. However, before we go further, we will look at some of the tools used in this book to allow you to follow along with a minimal number of questions about how something was achieved. In order to follow along with the code samples in this book, you will need to have the following on your development machine:

- **Sublime Text**–We will be setting up a custom build command so that you can simply transpile and execute your scripts using the default build command. You can get Sublime Text here.

- **NodeJS**–Please ensure that you have Node installed on your machine. You can get Node here.

- **Git client**–Please ensure that you have Git installed on your machine. You can get Git here.

- **Gist.run**–We will be using this website for most of our live examples. You can check it out here.

Most of the code samples will be building on skeleton navigation reference implementation or using Gist.run as our online playground.

 Note: Unless otherwise indicated, we are going to use Sublime Text as our development IDE and Google Chrome as our browser for debugging.

Browser support

Aurelia works well with all modern browsers; take a look here at which versions are supported. Throughout this book, we will be using Google Chrome as our default browser for both rendering and debugging our Aurelia applications.

Code listings

All code listings in the book have been generated using Sublime Text 3. Most of the code examples and screenshots were created using Google Chrome. Once you have your Aurelia application running, you should be able to simply make changes to your source code and save the file. The development workflow will automatically refresh your browser with the changes so that you can focus on development and not all the tasks related to building a web application.

For the majority of the working samples, we will be using https://gist.run. This will give you the ability to test out the samples without needing to set up your own project. I do walk you through setting up your own project, but this gives you the ability to decide which to use.

Aurelia CLI

Aurelia CLI is a command-line interface that allows you to configure your application with simple commands. In order to use the CLI, you need to ensure that you have all the dependencies installed from the "Getting set up" section.

Let's install Aurelia CLI by executing the following Node package manager command line to install it globally:

Code Listing 1

```
npm install -g aurelia-cli
```

Once you have this completed, navigate to the folder where you created your new project and execute the following command:

Code Listing 2

```
au new
```

You will see several prompts to help configure your new project. The following set of screenshots show what the interface looks like:

Figure 1: Aurelia CLI–au new

Enter a project name that you would like created.

Figure 2: Aurelia CLI–setup type

You can choose any of the selections, but we will select the **Custom** option to show you all the choices you have.

```
What transpiler would you like to use?

1. Babel (Default)
   An open source, standards-compliant ES2015 and ESNext transpiler.
2. TypeScript
   An open source, ESNext superset that adds optional strong typing.

> 1▊
```

Figure 3: Aurelia CLI–transpiler type

Here we select **Babel** as the transpiler, but you can choose TypeScript if you like.

```
What css processor would you like to use?

1. None (Default)
   Use standard CSS with no pre-processor.
2. Less
   Extends the CSS language, adding features that allow variables, mixins,
   functions and many other techniques.
3. Sass
   A mature, stable, and powerful professional grade CSS extension.
4. Stylus
   Expressive, dynamic and robust CSS.
5. Post CSS
   A tool for transforcing CSS with JavaScript.

> 1▊
```

Figure 4: Aurelia CLI–CSS processor

You have the opportunity to choose a CSS processor, or simply use standard CSS, as we have selected here.

```
Would you like to configure unit testing?

1. Yes (Default)
   Configure your app with Jasmine and Karma.
2. No
   Skip testing. My code is always perfect anyway.

> 1▊
```

Figure 5: Aurelia CLI–Unit Testing

You also have the option to elect to configure your project for unit testing.

```
What is your default code editor?

1. Visual Studio Code (Default)
   Code editing. Redefined. Free. Open source. Runs everywhere.
2. Atom
   A hackable text editor for the 21st Century.
3. Sublime
   A sophisticated text editor for code, markup and prose.
4. WebStorm
   A lightweight yet powerful IDE, perfectly equipped for complex
   client-side development.

> 1▊
```

Figure 6: Aurelia CLI–code editor

Next, you are presented with the ability to select which code editor you will use for the project.

```
Project Configuration

    Name: my-project
    Platform: Default
    Transpiler: Babel
    CSS Processor: None
    Unit Test Runner: Karma
    Editor: Visual Studio Code

Would you like to create this project?

1. Yes (Default)
   Creates the project structure based on your selections.
2. Restart
   Restarts the wizard, allowing you to make different selections.
3. Abort
   Aborts the new project wizard.

> 1
```

Figure 7: Aurelia CLI– review

Finally, you are presented with a project configuration and the ability to create the project, restart, or abort. After you press **Enter**, your project configuration is created. You should see something similar to the following screenshot:

Name		Date Modified
▶ aurelia_project		Today, 9:00 AM
favicon.ico		Today, 9:00 AM
index.html		Today, 9:00 AM
jsconfig.json		Today, 9:00 AM
karma.conf.js		Today, 9:00 AM
package.json		Today, 9:00 AM
▶ scripts		Today, 9:00 AM
▶ src		Today, 9:00 AM
▶ test		Today, 9:00 AM

Figure 8: Aurelia CLI–Project creation

```
Would you like to install the project dependencies?

1. Yes (Default)
   Installs all server, client and tooling dependencies needed to build
   the project.
2. No
   Completes the new project wizard without installing dependencies.

> 1
```

Figure 9: Aurelia CLI–Install project dependencies

Aurelia will ask you if you want to install the project dependencies. If you select **Yes**, it will go through and install all the dependencies for your project. If you select **No**, you can install them manually by entering the following command:

Code Listing 3

```
npm install
```

That's it! You can now run your new application by executing the following command:

Code Listing 4

```
au run
```

Auto browser refresh

If want your browser to automatically refresh after you have made changes to your source, you can execute the following instead:

Code Listing 5

```
au new --watch
```

Environments

The Aurelia CLI comes set up with three standard environments: `dev`, `stage`, and `prod`. If you wish to target a specific environment, you can do this by executing a command like the following:

Code Listing 6

```
au run --env stage --watch
```

In this case above, we are targeting the `stage` environment, but we could easily target `prod` or `dev`.

Bundling

When you use the Aurelia CLI, take note that it always bundles your code. You can force a bundle without running the application by executing the following command and specifying a target environment:

Code Listing 7

```
au build --env stage
```

Testing

If you have elected to include unit tests in your project, you can run your tests manually executing the following command:

Code Listing 8

```
au test
```

If you want to have your test run automatically, you can execute the following command:

Code Listing 9

```
au test -watch
```

Generators

Aurelia CLI comes with some great generators that help you with repetitive workflows. Execute the following command:

Code Listing 10

```
au generate <resource>
```

You can use any of the following values for **<resource>**:

- **element**
- **attribute**
- **value-converter**
- **binding-behavior**
- **task**
- **generator**

ASP.NET Core

It is possible to use Visual Studio and create an ASP.NET Core project, and then allow the Aurelia CLI to target this existing project for setup. To accomplish this, you first would need to navigate to the web project folder that contains the .xproj file. Here you execute the following command:

Code Listing 11

```
au new -here
```

Be sure to select **ASP.NET Core** when going through the prompts.

What else is there?

There are many more things you can do using the Aurelia CLI. The Aurelia team is rapidly updating the CLI to be even more friendly and powerful. Please refer to this link for more information on the Aurelia CLI.

If you get stuck or are not sure what version of the CLI you're using, you can use the following command to get the current version:

Code Listing 12

```
au -v
```

If you want to see which options are available using the CLI, execute the following command:

Code Listing 13

```
au help
```

ESNext and TypeScript

Aurelia gives you the flexibility to develop your application using the technologies that are most comfortable to you. Whether you want to use ES6 and ES7 or use TypeScript, there is an example project for you to look at.

We will use the Aurelia Skeleton Navigation project to clone from GitHub. You can also download the latest version from here if you like. The following are the steps required to clone the project from GitHub. Navigate to a folder where you would like to have the project cloned and execute the following command:

Code Listing 14

```
git clone git@github.com:aurelia/skeleton-navigation.git
```

This command assumes you have an SSH key and passphrase added to your account. Alternatively, if you'd rather use HTTPS, you can use the following command:

Code Listing 15

```
git clone https://github.com/aurelia/skeleton-navigation.git
```

Either command will clone the project in the folder where you executed. You should see the following after you navigate to the skeleton-navigation directory:

Code Listing 16

```
skeleton-navigation/
 circle.yml
 CONTRIBUTING.md
 ISSUE_TEMPLATE.md
 LICENSE
 README.md
 skeleton-esnext/
 skeleton-esnext-aspnetcore/
 skeleton-esnext-webpack/
 skeleton-typescript/
 skeleton-typescript-aspnetcore/
 skeleton-typescript-webpack/
```

Let's now take a look at the skeleton-esnext folder containing the JSPM implementation.

JSPM

JavaScript Package Manager (JSPM) is another means for configuring and setting up your Aurelia project.

Before you get started, you will need to ensure that you are in the skeleton-esnext folder. In order to use JSPM, you need to ensure that you have all the dependencies installed from the "Getting set up" section.

Let's install JSPM by executing the following command line and installing it globally:

Code Listing 17

```
npm install -g jspm
```

Now that we have JSPM installed and we have cloned the skeleton navigation project, we can navigate to either the skeleton-esnext or skeleton-typescript project. A quick way to tell if you are in a project that is configured to support JSPM is to look for the config.js file. Let's navigate to the **skeleton-esnext** project and execute the following command:

Code Listing 18

```
npm install
```

This will resolve all of our dependencies as specified in our package.json file.

Next, execute the following command to bring in all of our JSPM dependencies:

Code Listing 19

```
jspm install -y
```

> *Note: The -y flag indicates to skip prompts and use default inputs during the installation.*

You are now ready to start the application locally. Execute the following command to launch the server:

Code Listing 20

```
gulp watch
```

Now, simply browse to the following URL: http://localhost:9000/.

Unit tests

You will need to be sure that you have Karma CLI installed before you can run any tests. Execute the following command to install it:

Code Listing 21

```
npm install -g karma-cli
```

Now, you will be able to run your tests using the following command:

Code Listing 22

```
gulp test
```

E2E tests

All integration tests utilize <u>Protractor</u>. You will need to be sure that you have the necessary webdriver installed before you can run any tests. Execute the following command to install it:

Code Listing 23

```
gulp webdriver-update
```

Next, you will need to configure the path to the webdriver and adjust the `seleniumServerJar` property to the correct version number inside the protractor.conf.js file. Refer to the Protractor documentation for more information.

All of your tests need to reside in the following location from the root of your application:

Code Listing 24

```
test/e2e/src
```

You are now ready to run your application and run tests. It takes two separate console instances to perform these. First, run your application by executing the following command:

Code Listing 25

```
gulp watch
```

Next, execute your tests in another console:

Code Listing 26

```
gulp e2e
```

That's it!

Webpack

If you don't want to have to deal with both `npm` and `jspm`, then `webpack` might be just what you are looking for. Be sure that you followed all the steps to get your dependencies installed from the "Getting set up" section.

Since we have already cloned the skeleton navigation project, we can navigate to either the skeleton-esnext-webpack or the skeleton-typescript-webpack project. Let's navigate to the **skeleton-esnext-webpack** project and execute the following command:

Code Listing 27

```
npm install
```

This will resolve all of our dependencies as specified in our package.json file.

You are now ready to start the application locally. Execute the following to launch the server:

Code Listing 28

```
npm start
```

Now, simply browse to the following URL: http://localhost:9000/.

Bundling

To create a bundle, execute the following command:

Code Listing 29

```
npm run build
```

If you would like your bundle to be production-ready, execute the following:

Code Listing 30

```
npm run build:prod
```

To test either of your builds, execute the following:

Code Listing 31

```
npm run server:prod
```

If you're watching your project file structure, you might have noticed that a new folder was created during this process. You now have a dist folder that contains all the dependencies for deployment.

Unit tests

To run unit tests, you can execute the following command:

Code Listing 32

```
npm test
```

E2E tests

All of the integration tests use Protractor.

All of your tests need to reside in the following location from the root of your application:

Code Listing 33

```
test/e2e/src
```

You are now ready to run your application and run tests, so execute the following command:

Code Listing 34

```
npm run e2e
```

There may be times when you want to run your tests manually. You can do this using the following command:

Code Listing 35

```
WEBPACK_PORT=19876 npm start
```

This gets the server running and ready for tests to be called from another console instance.

Execute the following command in another console instance once you have a bundle ready:

Code Listing 36

```
npm run e2e:start
```

That's it!

ASP.NET Core

If you come from a Microsoft background and find Visual Studio to be your best friend, then you are not alone. We have already learned that we can use Aurelia CLI to accomplish this, but the skeleton navigation doesn't leave us wanting, either.

Because we have already cloned the skeleton navigation project, we can navigate to either the skeleton-esnext-aspnetcore or skeleton-typescript-aspnetcore project. Let's navigate to the **skeleton-esnext-aspnetcore** project. You will notice that this folder contains a Visual Studio solution, and there is another folder named src/skeleton.

Let's navigate to the **src/skeleton** and see what it takes to get our application ready for development. First, we are going to need to ensure that we have both `gulp` and `jspm` installed. We can achieve this by executing the following command:

Code Listing 37

```
npm install -g jspm gulp
```

Running in Visual Studio 2015

You will need to have Visual Studio 2015 with Update 3 or later in order to run the application.

You will also need to have ASP.NET Core downloaded and installed. You can find instructions on how to do this here.

1. Open the solution file **skeleton-esnext-aspnetcore.sln**. Visual Studio will automatically run `npm install` and `jspm install` when you first open the solution. It is possible to rerun the commands at any time using a command prompt inside the **src/skeleton** folder.

2. Inside Visual Studio, open the **Task Runner Explorer**, and you should see the tasks runner report that the `gulp watch` command is running.

3. Press **F5** or click **Run**, and Visual Studio will launch your default browser and navigate to the correct URL.

Running without Visual Studio 2015

It is possible to develop your Aurelia application using ASP.NET Core without Visual Studio 2015. For example, you could develop your application using Visual Studio Code.

You will also need to have the ASP.NET Core downloaded and installed. You can find instructions on how to do this here.

The following are the steps required to get your application running:

1. Resolve your `npm` and `jspm` dependencies.

Code Listing 38

```
npm install
```

This handles all of the dependencies in your `package.json` as well as executing the following command as identified by the `postinstall` entry:

Code Listing 39

```
jspm install -y
```

 Note: Some Windows users have experienced an error, "unknown command unzip." This can be resolved by executing the following: `npm install -g unzip`. Next, rerun the following command: `jspm install`.

2. Build the project using the following command:

Code Listing 40

```
gulp build
dotnet build
```

3. Next, execute the following command:

Code Listing 41

```
dotnet restore
```

4. Run the application by executing the following:

Code Listing 42

```
dotnet run
```

5. If you wish to have your coding changes reflected in the browser automatically, execute the following command in a second console instance:

Code Listing 43

```
gulp watch
```

6. Now, simply browse to the following URL: http://localhost:5000.

Bundling

Bundling is performed by the Aurelia Bundler. A `gulp` task has already been configured, and you can create a bundle by executing the following command:

Code Listing 44

```
gulp bundle
```

It is possible to unbundle using the following command:

Code Listing 45

```
gulp unbundle
```

To test the bundled application, execute the following:

Code Listing 46

```
gulp serve-bundle
```

If you are curious as to how the bundles are configured, you can look at the **bundles.js** file.

Unit tests

You will need to be sure that you have Karma CLI installed before you can run any tests. Execute the following command to install it:

Code Listing 47

```
npm install -g karma-cli
```

Next, you will need to install Aurelia libs for test visibility. Execute the following command:

Code Listing 48

```
jspm install aurelia-framework
jspm install aurelia-http-client
jspm install aurelia-router
```

Now, you will be able to run your tests using the following command:

Code Listing 49

```
karma start
```

E2E (End-to-End) tests

All integration tests utilize Protractor. You will need to be sure that you have the necessary webdriver installed before you can run any tests. Execute the following command to install it:

Code Listing 50

```
gulp webdriver-update
```

Next, you will need to configure the path to the webdriver and adjust the `seleniumServerJar` property to the correct version number inside the

protractor.conf.js file. Refer to the Protractor documentation for more information.

All of your tests need to reside in the following location from the root of your application:

Code Listing 51

```
test/e2e/src
```

You are now ready to run your application and run tests. It takes two separate console instances to perform this. First, run your application by executing the following command:

Code Listing 52

```
gulp watch
```

Next, execute your tests in another console:

Code Listing 53

```
gulp e2e
```

That's it!

Exporting your bundled production version

A `gulp` task is already configured to allow you to export your application bundled and ready for production. Execute the following command:

Code Listing 54

```
gulp export
```

This will export your application into the Export folder ready for deployment.

Chapter 3 ES6 and ES7

Overview

In Chapter 2, we looked at getting your development environment set up how you want it—with Aurelia, we have many options and choices. In this chapter, we are going to be looking at the skeleton navigation and evaluating all the moving pieces. You can either follow along with the setup that you liked best from Chapter 2, or you can follow along from the Git repository for this book that has a project dedicated for each chapter. Before we dig into any Aurelia-specific features, it is necessary to talk about some new programming paradigms that we get from ES6 and ES7. We will then look at some dependency injection and how it is useful. Finally, we will look at decorators and async/await features.

A look at ES6 and ES7

Aurelia gives you the ability to develop your applications using ES6 and ES7 features natively using transpiling or Microsoft TypeScript. We will be looking at ES6 and ES7 capabilities in this book, but be aware that you also have the option of using TypeScript. Below is a list of some of the features we get while developing applications in Aurelia:

- Classes
- Scoping
- Templates
- String interpolation
- Decorators
- Async/await

All the features of ES6 and ES7 deserve their own dedicated book, and you can check out *ES6 Succinctly* here if you are interested in what it brings to the table. We will cover each of the listed items briefly to get you up and running.

Classes

If you are familiar with developing in Java or C#, then you will be very comfortable with the concept of classes. In the new JavaScript (ES6), this is a nice added feature that allows us to maintain a clean separation of concerns with very little ceremony. Before we had classes, we had to use the revealing module pattern to ensure that we were not polluting the global namespace. Let's take a look at what a class looks like in JavaScript:

Code Listing 55

```
class Welcome {
  constructor() {
  }
}
```

This syntax is clean and simple.

Scoping

Another long-awaited feature is better scoping in JavaScript. In ES5, regardless of whether our variables were declared inside functions or blocks, they would be hoisted to the top block level, and this would cause a lot of problems. We now have a new keyword, `let`, and this gives us true block-level scoping. Consider the following:

Code Listing 56

```
class Welcome {
 constructor() {
 this.result = 0;
 }

 add(first, second) {
 let result = -1;

 if (first && second) {
  let result = first + second;
 }

 return result;
 }
}
```

Before we go on and use this class and the `add` function, let's look at what we have created here. In ES5, this could potentially cause a lot of headaches and problems. We are defining a class-level variable inside the constructor called `result`. Next, we create a function-level variable called `result` and initialize it to -1. We then create a block-level variable and initialize it to the first and second variables. Finally, we return the variable `result` back from the function.

Let's now write a little code to test this class and see what happens:

Code Listing 57

```
let w = new Welcome();
console.log(w.add(1,2)); // -1
console.log(w.result); // 0
```

Our code is now more consistent and behaves as would be expected. You can see that the `add` function returns -1 when we call it. You can also see that when we access the class-level variable, we get 0 back.

Template strings

Strings in JavaScript have always been a pain, and have always been limited when compared to other mature languages. Template strings change this completely and give us a lot of power with our string manipulation. Some of the chief features are:

- String interpolation
- Embedded expressions
- Multiline strings

Before we look at any of these new features, we must learn the pattern for creating template strings. Consider the following:

Code Listing 58

```
let message = `Hello World`;
```

This simple example introduces the use of backticks (`) instead of single or double quotes. That is all there is to template strings. Let's now look at how we can use them.

String interpolation

String interpolation gives us the ability to substitute values within our template strings with variables. Let's look at the following example:

Code Listing 59

```
let fname = 'Matt';
let lname = 'Duffield';
let message = `Hello ${fname} ${lname}, how are you?`;
```

When we execute this script, we get: "Hello Matt Duffield, how are you?"

Embedded expressions

Embedded expressions allow us to embed JavaScript expressions in our template strings. Consider the following example:

Code Listing 60

```
let three = 3;
let four = 4;
let message = `The product of 3 x 4 is ${three*four}`;
```

When we execute this script, we get: "The product of 3 x 4 is 12". We can call functions and even access members off of our objects, as well.

Multiline strings

Multiline strings are by far one of the most awaited features of ES6, as they give us cleaner syntax when trying to author multiline content. Let's look at the following example:

Code Listing 61

```
let user = 'Matt';

let message = `Thank you ${user} for contact the support team!

We value your business and are more than happy to answer any questi
ons you may have.`;
```

 Note: The creators of Aurelia wisely chose to use the same syntax notation for their databinding engine.

Decorators

Decorators allow us to annotate pieces of code to help reduce redundancies. Consider the following example of how we use decorators for dependency injection:

Code Listing 62

```
import {inject} from 'aurelia-framework';

import {DataService} from 'services/data-service';


@inject(DataService)

class Customer {

 constructor(dataService) {

 this.dataService = dataService;

 }


 ...

}
```

You will see other advantages of using decorators when working with TypeScript in Aurelia, as well. If you wish to use dependency injection without the `inject` decorator, you can write it out as follows:

Code Listing 63

```
import {DataService} from 'services/data-service';


class Customer {
```

```
static inject = [DataService];

constructor(dataService) {
this.dataService = dataService;
}


...

}
```

As you get more comfortable with Aurelia, you will see uses of decorators throughout the framework and in plugins.

 Note: By default, Aurelia handles all dependencies as singletons. You can change this by decorating your class with the @transient decorator.

Async/await

Writing code that allows you to make asynchronous calls while keeping the code clean has long plagued JavaScript users. Using libraries and promises, we have come closer, but now with `async` and `await` coming in ES7, we are getting a paradigm that makes asynchronous programming much less difficult. First, let's look at how we currently implement our logic without `async` and `await`:

Code Listing 64

```
import {DataService} from 'services/data-service';

class Customer {
static inject = [DataService];
data = [];

constructor(dataService) {
this.dataService = dataService;
}

activate() {
return this.dataService.getCustomers()
.then(response => {
```

```
    this.data = resonse.json();
  });
  }
}
```

If we return a promise from the `activate` function part of the screen lifecycle, Aurelia will wait until the call returns and executes the `then` callback before binding to the screen. We will go into Aurelia's screen activation lifecycle later, but this is a common scenario and needs to be shown so you can see the differences in implementation. Now, let's look at the same implementation using `async` and `await`:

Code Listing 65

```
import {DataService} from 'services/data-service';

class Customer {
  static inject = [DataService];
  data = [];

  constructor(dataService) {
    this.dataService = dataService;
  }

  async activate() {
    let response = await this.dataService.getCustomers();
    this.data = await response.json();
  }
}
```

We are effectively doing exactly the same thing. In fact, Babel will transpile this code to look pretty much like the first example. This is much cleaner and helps reduce the madness involved writing a lot asynchronous code.

Chapter 4 Skeleton Navigation

Overview

Up until now, we have been talking about getting things set up and general development in JavaScript. Let's dive into the focus of this book and take a look at the skeleton navigation. We will evaluate and look at what it takes to create an Aurelia application.

Skeleton Navigation demo

We will be using the **skeleton-esnext-webpack** version. You can start the server by executing the following command:

Code Listing 66

```
npm start
```

Next, open up your favorite browser and navigate to the following URL:
http://localhost:9000.

The application will spin for a second, and then you should see the following:

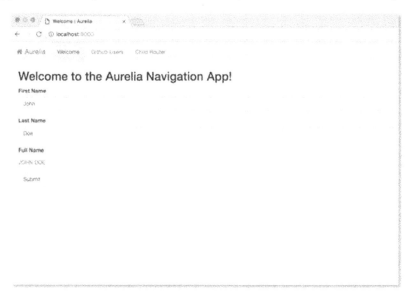

Figure 10: Skeleton Navigation

From this simple site, we will be able to start understanding how Aurelia works and how we can use it for our own applications.

Let's look a little more at the Welcome page. We can intuit that we have two-way databinding and a computed property. If I were to use the first and last name input box fields to input "Matt Duffield," I would get the following screenshot:

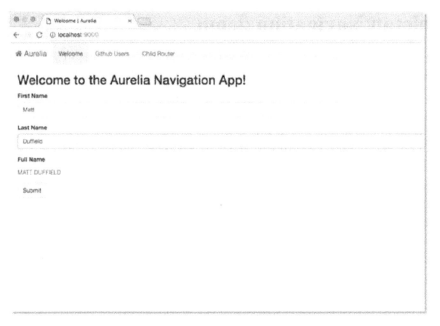

Figure 11: Demonstrating two-way databinding

 Note: If you click on the Aurelia menu item on the far left, you will be redirected to the default page, which is the Welcome screen.

We also see that we have a **Submit** button, and when we click on it, we get the following output:

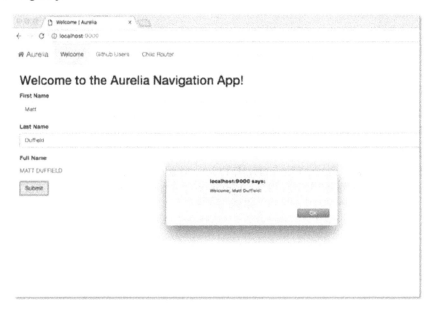

Figure 12: Demonstrating click delegate

Moving on, we see that we have a menu at the top that allows us to navigate to other pages. Let's see what we get when we click on **Github Users**:

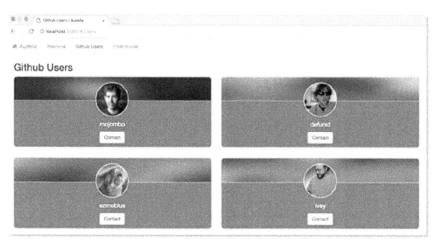

Figure 13: Demonstrating Web API call

As we will see in a later chapter, this page demonstrates making a Web API call and rendering the results to the screen.

Finally, let's navigate to the **Child Router** menu item and repeat a couple times. You should see something similar to Figure 14:

Figure 14: Demonstrating routing capabilities

If we consider what is happening here, we see that we are able to easily have a powerful hierarchical routing system. We will look at what it takes to perform this in a later chapter.

Skeleton Navigation architecture

We have seen how the application runs and behaves. Let's take a look at what it takes to build the application. We will start by looking at the file structure of the project:

Figure 15: Skeleton Navigation file structure

As you can see, all of our application source code is under the src folder. We also have another folder for our styles. We have a test folder that will give us examples of both unit and end-to-end testing. Finally, we have our root location where our index.html file resides.

 The structure of the skeleton navigation varies slightly depending on which project example you choose to evaluate.

index.html

Let's start by looking at the index.html file:

```
1  <!DOCTYPE html>
2  <html>
3    <head>
4      <title><%- webpackConfig.metadata.title %></title>
5      <meta name="viewport" content="width=device-width, initial-scale=1">
6      <base href="<%- webpackConfig.metadata.baseUrl %>">
7      <!-- imported CSS are concatenated and added automatically -->
8    </head>
9    <body aurelia-app="main">
10     <div class="splash">
11       <div class="message"><%- webpackConfig.metadata.title %></div>
12       <i class="fa fa-spinner fa-spin"></i>
13     </div>
14     <% if (webpackConfig.metadata.ENV === 'development') { %>
15     <!-- Webpack Dev Server reload -->
16     <script src="/webpack-dev-server.js"></script>
17     <% } %>
18   </body>
19 </html>
20
```

Figure 16: index.html

Inside our index.html file, we see that we are setting the title of our application by pulling it from the `webpackConfig.metadata.title` property. Next, we set the meta establishing our width and initial scale. Finally, we set the base tag `href` to the `webpackConfig.metadata.baseUrl` property.

Inside the body, we see our first references to Aurelia proper. We see the `aurelia-app` attribute with the value `main`. This lets Aurelia know that the entry point for our application will be to look for a file name, `main.js`. We can confirm that this is the case by finding the main.js file under the **src** folder in the Figure 6–Skeleton Navigation file structure.

Inside the body definition, we see a `div` that contains a class with the value `splash`. The `div` contains child elements with the title of our application contained in the `webpackConfig.metadata.title` property, and also a reference to Font Awesome for displaying a busy indicator. This `div` will become visible as our application loads a given screen. Once the activate function has returned, the `div` will then become hidden.

The last markup you see has a conditional requirement to only be utilized if our **ENV** has the value of `development`. If our **ENV** contains the value `development`, then we will be able to develop our application in our favorite editor, and when we save our files, the application in the browser will automatically refresh.

main.js

Now that we understand what is happening in the index.html file, let's take a look at the main.js file and see what is happening there. Consider the following:

```
1  // we want font-awesome to load as soon as possible to show the fa-spinner
2  import '../styles/styles.css';
3  import 'font-awesome/css/font-awesome.css';
4  import 'bootstrap/dist/css/bootstrap.css';
5  import 'bootstrap';
6
7  // comment out if you don't want a Promise polyfill (remove also from webpack.common.js)
8  import * as Bluebird from 'bluebird';
9  Bluebird.config({ warnings: false });
10
11 export async function configure(aurelia) {
12   aurelia.use
13     .standardConfiguration()
14     .developmentLogging();
15
16   // Uncomment the line below to enable animation.
17   // aurelia.use.plugin('aurelia-animator-css');
18   // if the css animator is enabled, add swap-order="after" to all router-view elements
19
20   // Anyone wanting to use HTMLImports to load views, will need to install the following plugin.
21   // aurelia.use.plugin('aurelia-html-import-template-loader')
22
23   await aurelia.start();
24   aurelia.setRoot('app');
25
26   // if you would like your website to work offline (Service Worker),
27   // install and enable the @easy-webpack/config-offline package
28   // in webpack.config.js and uncomment the following code:
29   /*
30   const offline = await System.import('offline-plugin/runtime');
31   offline.install();
32   */
33 }
```

Figure 17: main.js

Starting from the top of the file, we see five `import` statements. This is new to ES6, and module loading allows us to ensure separation of concerns. We see that we are importing `style.css`, `font-awesome.css`, `bootstrap.css`, and finally, `bootstrap`. The first three references are CSS files, and the last one is the actual Twitter Bootstrap reference by the name `bootstrap`. We can verify that there exists an entry called `bootstrap` by looking quickly at our package.json file. Let's look at a portion of this file now:

```
60   "bugs": {
61     "url": "https://github.com/aurelia/skeleton-navigation/issues"
62   },
63   "homepage": "https://github.com/aurelia/skeleton-navigation#readme",
64   "aurelia": {
65     "build": {
66       "resources": []
67     }
68   },
69   "dependencies": {
70     "aurelia-bootstrapper-webpack": "^1.0.0",
71     "aurelia-event-aggregator": "^1.0.0",
72     "aurelia-fetch-client": "^1.0.0",
73     "aurelia-framework": "^1.0.0",
74     "aurelia-history-browser": "^1.0.0",
75     "aurelia-loader-webpack": "^1.0.0",
76     "aurelia-logging-console": "^1.0.0",
77     "aurelia-pal-browser": "^1.0.0",
78     "aurelia-polyfills": "^1.0.0",
79     "aurelia-route-recognizer": "^1.0.0",
80     "aurelia-router": "^1.0.2",
81     "aurelia-templating-binding": "^1.0.0",
82     "aurelia-templating-resources": "^1.0.0",
83     "aurelia-templating-router": "^1.0.0",
84     "bluebird": "^3.4.1",
85     "bootstrap": "^3.3.7",
86     "font-awesome": "^4.6.3",
87     "isomorphic-fetch": "^2.2.1",
88     "jquery": "^3.1.0"
89   },
```

We see from the snippet that our package.json file does contain an entry named **bootstrap** in the **dependencies** section. This name is what we use in our **import** statements, and you see that we bring in **bluebird** the same way. With Bluebird imported, we call its **config** function, passing in a JSON literal.

Next, we export a configure function and mark it as **async**. The function receives an Aurelia object as its parameter, and we use this object to configure our application.

On our **aurelia** object, we specify we want to **use** the **standardConfiguration** and turn on **developmentLogging**.

We make sure that we **await** the call to **aurelia.start()** so that we can set the root entry for the application to the value **app**. You will see that this value corresponds to the app.html and app.js in our src folder.

There are quite a few comments in this file, and we will come back to and look at how they are used in later chapters.

app.html and app.js

We are slowly unraveling how Aurelia performs its startup sequence. We now move on to our first view and view-model in the application. Let's take a look at the app.html file:

Figure 19: app.html

Every screen or page that is defined in Aurelia starts with a template tag containing all of the markup. Next, you will see a **require** tag that allows us to bring in custom elements. We immediately use the **nav-bar** custom element and bind the router property to a **router** object on our view-model, which we will see shortly.

After this, we see a **div** that contains a single class, **page-host**. Inside our **div** is an Aurelia custom element, **router-view**. It is through this element that we are able to inject our pages into this location.

Let's look at the app.js file next:

```
1   export class App {
2     configureRouter(config, router) {
3       config.title = 'Aurelia';
4       config.map([
5         { route: ['', 'welcome'], name: 'welcome',      moduleId: './welcome',      nav: true, title: 'Welcome' },
6         { route: 'users',         name: 'users',        moduleId: './users',        nav: true, title: 'Github Users' },
7         { route: 'child-router',  name: 'child-router', moduleId: './child-router', nav: true, title: 'Child Router' }
8       ]);
9
10      this.router = router;
11    }
12  }
13
```

Figure 20: app.js

By convention, when we load our app.html file, Aurelia tries to find a corresponding view-model class with the same naming convention, but with the extension .js. We see that this file defines a class named **App**, and it has a single function, **configureRouter**, that takes in a **config** and **router** object.

The **config** object allows us to specify a **title** for our application. It is this title that shows up in the menu besides the home icon. We also provide an array to the **map** function. This array corresponds to the routes we wish to define in our application. Looking at the first entry in the array, we see a **route** property that has two entries: **''** and **welcome**. This is how we are specifying our default route so that Aurelia knows which route to display when no route is passed, or when an invalid route is passed. We also have **name, moduleId, nav,** and **title**. We will look more carefully at the router in a later chapter.

Finally, we set the passed-in **router** object to a class-level property with the same name.

nav-bar.html

When we were looking at the app.html file, we required in a custom element, **nav-bar.html**. When Aurelia sees this tag, it will look for the nav-bar.html file relative to the app.html file. Let's take a quick look at what was involved in creating this first custom element:

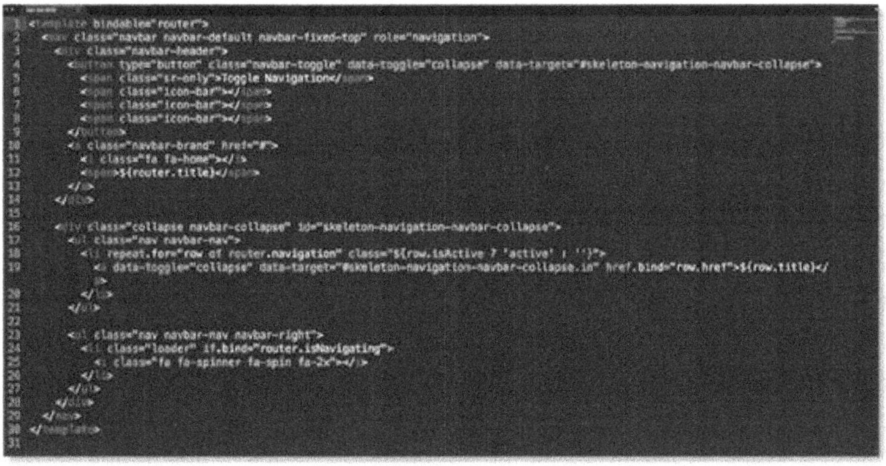

```html
<template bindable="router">
  <nav class="navbar navbar-default navbar-fixed-top" role="navigation">
    <div class="navbar-header">
      <button type="button" class="navbar-toggle" data-toggle="collapse" data-target="#skeleton-navigation-navbar-collapse">
        <span class="sr-only">Toggle Navigation</span>
        <span class="icon-bar"></span>
        <span class="icon-bar"></span>
        <span class="icon-bar"></span>
      </button>
      <a class="navbar-brand" href="#">
        <i class="fa fa-home"></i>
        <span>${router.title}</span>
      </a>
    </div>

    <div class="collapse navbar-collapse" id="skeleton-navigation-navbar-collapse">
      <ul class="nav navbar-nav">
        <li repeat.for="row of router.navigation" class="${row.isActive ? 'active' : ''}">
          <a data-toggle="collapse" data-target="#skeleton-navigation-navbar-collapse.in" href.bind="row.href">${row.title}</a>
        </li>
      </ul>

      <ul class="nav navbar-nav navbar-right">
        <li class="loader" if.bind="router.isNavigating">
          <i class="fa fa-spinner fa-spin fa-2x"></i>
        </li>
      </ul>
    </div>
  </nav>
</template>
```

Figure 21: nav-bar.html

If you have played with Twitter Bootstrap, you will see that what is presented here is a Bootstrap menu with some Aurelia bindings. We will go into databinding in much more detail in the next chapter, but there are a couple things to note about this custom element. First, if you refer back to Figure 6, you will notice that there is no corresponding view-model file name, nav-bar.js. This is an example of a custom element that does not need any custom behavior defined in a view-model, and Aurelia is happy to provide a generic default view-model for such scenarios. Also notice that on the **`template`** tag, we see a **`bindable`** attribute. This lets Aurelia know that this custom element expects to have a property exposed on the view-model named **`router`**, and that you can bind to it.

That's it for now! We will move right into databinding in the next chapter, so stay tuned.

Chapter 5 Databinding

Overview

One of the most important features to a framework is the ability to provide some form of databinding, and Aurelia has a wonderful and mature implementation. We will first look at the core components of databinding, and then dive into real world scenarios. Let's get started.

Bind

In Aurelia, it is possible to bind to practically any attribute, with a few exceptions. You achieve this by using the following markup:

Code Listing 67

```
<input value.bind="firstname" />
```

This simple example demonstrates how to "bind" to a given attribute of an element. Here, we are binding to the value property of the input control.

 Note: Binding is typically one-way, but if your element is inside a form tag, then the binding will actually be two-way by default.

If we go back to the `nav-bar.html` file, we can see another example of a usage of bind:

```
23    <ul class="nav navbar-nav navbar-right">
24        <li class="loader" if.bind="router.isNavigating">
25            <i class="fa fa-spinner fa-spin fa-2x"></i>
26        </li>
27    </ul>
```

Figure 22: if.bind example

Here, we see an example of binding to an attribute that does not exist on the `li` element. The `if` attribute is provided by the Aurelia framework to allow us to programmatically add and remove *DOM* elements. The `if.bind` will inject the `li` element and its corresponding children when the expression `router.isNavigating` is `true`.

Perhaps you want the element to always be a part of the DOM, but to be hidden at times. You can do this by simply changing the binding to the following:

Code Listing 68

```
<li class="loader" show.bind="router.isNavigating">...</li>
```

By using `show.bind`, we are basically setting the style attribute to `display="none"`.

One-way

There are times when we just want our pages to reflect what is stored in our view-model and update whenever a value changes. That is exactly what one-way does for us. A simple example of this would be the following:

Code Listing 69

```
<li content.one-way="name"></li>
```

In this example, we are setting the content attribute of the `li` to be bound to the `name` property on our view-model. Whenever our `name` property changes, the `li` will be updated correspondingly.

Two-way

Likewise, if we want to be able to provide the ability for a binding to receive updates from the view-model as well as send updates from the view, we would need to create a binding like the following:

Code Listing 70

```
<input value.two-way="search" />
```

In this example, we are specifying that we want our `value` property of the `input` element to have two-way databinding so that changes in the view and view-model are reflected properly. Remember that if you are binding input and select elements inside a form tag, you will get two-way databinding automatically.

One-time

There may be times when you want to bind a value to a screen and you know that the value will never change in the view-model. You can notify Aurelia that it does not need to observe changes to this underlying property on the view-model and simply request it to render the initial value when the screen is loaded. If you change the value on the view-model at a later time, the view will not receive this update automatically. See the following for an example:

Code Listing 71

```
<span content.one-time="message"></span>
```

String interpolation

We just saw how to do a one-way binding, but you will find a lot of scenarios when you want to provide both content and a binding. This is where string interpolation comes in. The nice thing about this feature is that it is exactly the same as the ES6 specification, so you are not learning anything new from an API perspective. Consider the following example from the `nav-bar.html` custom element:

```
10        <a class="navbar-brand" href="#">
11            <i class="fa fa-home"></i>
12            <span>${router.title}</span>
13        </a>
14    </div>
```

Figure 23: String interpolation snippet

In this snippet, we see that this portion of the markup corresponds to what will be displayed in the left-most entry of the menu. If we refer to Figure 11, we see that there is a `title` property. It is this property that we are going to interpolate when we load the screen; we can add content around it and customize our output like the following:

Code Listing 72

```
<span>Hello ${name}, how are you doing?</span>
```

Here you can see that we have a dynamic message we are displaying in our `span` element. Let's look at another example, this time using an expression:

Code Listing 73

```
<li class="${row.isActive ? 'active' : ''}">...</li>
```

In this example, we are adding the `isActive` class to the `li` element when the `row.isActive` property is `true`.

Loops

Binding to properties is great, but it really doesn't help when you need to loop over a collection of data. Aurelia has a great solution for this using the `repeat.for` syntax. Consider the following example taken again from the `nav-bar` custom element:

```
<li repeat.for="row of router.navigation"
    class="${row.isActive ? 'active' : ''}">
  <a data-toggle="collapse"
     data-target="#skeleton-navigation-navbar-collapse.in"
     href.bind="row.href">${row.title}</a>
</li>
```

Figure 24: repeat.for example

Here, we are looping over the `navigation` array property off of the `router` object. We can interpret the syntax as such:

For each row in the `navigation` array, inject the `li` element with its corresponding children.

Also notice that we can reference the `row` property within the child elements and access other properties. You can see that we access the `isActive`, `href`, and `title` properties this way.

 Note: If you need to reference something that is not in the context of the row object, you need to use the $parent keyword to go to the parent of the row object.

Ref binding

Sometimes you just want to bind to a property on another element. Aurelia makes this extremely easy to accomplish with the `ref` keyword. Consider the following example:

Code Listing 74

```
<template>
 <h1>${title}</h1>
 <input ref="customerName">
 <h2>Hello ${customerName.value}, how can I help you?</h2>
</template>
```

Here, we are referencing the input element and accessing the `value` property so that we can display its value in the span element. Not only do we have the ability to reference any element that has a `ref` attribute, but we can also reference it from the view-model.

Here is what we get for the output:

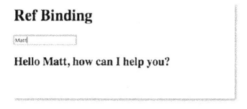

Figure 25: Ref Binding

You can see this example in action here.

Referencing functions

There will be times when you are authoring your screens and custom elements and attributes will have a bound property on your view-model that is looking for a reference to a function. If you were to use **bind** as the keyword against your function, you would not be guaranteed that the context of the **this** keyword would be correct. Most of the time, you will want **this** to be in the context of the view-model, and that is exactly what the **call** keyword does for you. Consider the following **saveButton** custom element template:

Code Listing 75

```
<template>
  <button click.delegate="saveFunc()">Save</button>
<template>
```

If we look at the markup above, we see a **bindable** property exposed from our view-model, named **saveFunc**. This property will now hold a reference to any **save** implementation using the **call** keyword, as we will see shortly. This is powerful in that it lets us create some generic solutions for common use cases, and yet pass in custom functionality like the **save** function to our custom elements.

Let's see what the view-model would look like for this custom element:

Code Listing 76

```
import {customElement, bindable} from 'aurelia-framework';


@customElement('save-button')

export class SaveButton {


  @bindable saveFunc;


  constructor() {
  }

}
```

Next, let's look at how we would use this:

Code Listing 77

```
<template>
  <require from='save-button'></require>
```

```
<h1>${title}</h1>
<save-button save-func.call="performSave()"></save-button>
</template>
```

By using the **call** keyword, we are passing a reference to the **performSave** function, and this ensures that the function is not executed immediately.

Let's look at the view-model and see what we have there:

Code Listing 78

```
export class App {
  title = 'Custom Element referencing a function';

  constuctor() {

  }

  performSave() {
  alert('You clicked save!');
  }
}
```

Our **performSave** function doesn't do much except throw up an alert when called. Finally, here is how it looks when we click **Save**:

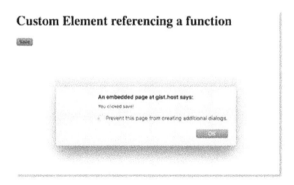

Figure 26: Custom Element referencing a function

You can see this example in action here.

We will be going into more detail on custom elements and attributes in a later chapter.

Event binding

Binding to properties and arrays and other elements is great, but sometimes you need to have some form of interaction with the user. A common scenario is performing some form of action when a user clicks on button or anchor tag. Aurelia supports binding to DOM events using the following formats:

- `click.delegate="sayHello()"`
- `click.trigger="sayHello()"`

The `delegate` keyword attaches a single event handler to the document that handles all events of that given type and dispatches them to the correct target when the corresponding event is raised.

The `trigger` keyword creates an event handler directly to the underlying element. When the event is fired, only the function reference will be invoked.

 Note: You can bind to any event in the DOM by removing the on *prefix and providing the rest of the event name in lowercase.*

Consider the following view snippet:

Code Listing 79

```
<template>
  <h1>${title}</h1>
  <input value.bind="name">
  <button click.delegate="sayHello()">Greeting</button>
</template>
```

In this simple example, we are binding the `click` event that will execute the `sayHello` function whenever a user clicks the button.

Here is what the `sayHello` function might look like in the view-model:

Code Listing 80

```
export class App {
  title = 'Event Binding';
  name = '';


  constuctor() {
```

```
  }

sayHello() {
alert(`Hello ${this.name}`);
  }
}
```

You can see this example in action here.

All event bindings come with an **$event** property that you can pass on to the view-model or use in your expression as follows:

Code Listing 81

```
<input ref="customerName" />
<button click.delegate="save($event.target, customerName.value)">
  Save
</button>
<button click.trigger="cancel($event)">Cancel</button>
```

This provides a lot of flexibility, and in a simple, elegant semantic. In general, you should use **delegate** rather than **trigger**. Event delegation improves application performance; it can reduce the number of event subscriptions by leveraging the "bubbling" characteristic of many events. With event delegation, handlers are not attached to individual elements.

Form controls

As I've already indicated, elements inside a form tag have their default binding as two-way. This section will cover both input bindings and select control bindings.

Input binding

The following is an example of input bindings:

Code Listing 82

```
<template>
 <form>
 <label>Customer Email</label>
 <input type="email" value.bind="customerEmail">
 <label>User Name</label>
 <input type="text" value.bind="username">
 </form>
</template>
```

Check-box binding

The most common scenario is binding a check box to a Boolean value. The following is an example of binding a `checkbox` to the property `billingAddressSameAsCustomerAddress` on the view-model:

Code Listing 83

```
<template>
 <form>
 <h4>Favorite Color</h4>
 <input type="checkbox"
  checked.bind="billingAddressSameAsCustomerAddress">
 </form>
</template>
```

It is also possible to bind to numbers, objects, and strings. You can find examples of each of these here.

Radio-button binding

Radio buttons are another common pattern that allow an end user to make a single selection from a list of options. The following is an example of binding radio buttons:

Code Listing 84

```
<template>
 <form>
 <h4>Favorite Color</h4>
 <label><input type="radio" name="color"
  value="red" checked.bind="selectedColor">Red</label>
 <label><input type="radio" name="color"
  value="blue" checked.bind="selectedColor">Blue</label>
 <label><input type="radio" name="color"
  value="green" checked.bind="selectedColor">Green</label>
 <br />
 Selected color: ${selectedColor}
 </form>
</template>
```

Again, it is also possible to bind to numbers, objects, and Booleans, aside from the string example shown above. You can find examples of each of these here.

Select binding

The `select` control allows users to perform a single or multiple selection. You indicate multiple selection by including the `multiple` attribute. Let's take a look at the following example:

Code Listing 85

```
<template>
 <form>
 <label>T-Shirt Size:<br />
  <select value.bind="shirtSize">
  <option repeat.for="size of sizes"
   model.bind="size.value">${size.name}
```

```
  </option>
  </select>
 </label>
 Shirt Size: ${shirtSize}
 </form>
</template>
```

Just like check boxes and radio buttons, it is possible to bind to numbers, objects, and strings. You can find examples of each of these here.

Let's see how this would look with the **multiple** attribute on the **select** control:

Code Listing 86

```
<template>
 <form>
 <label>College Courses:<br />
  <select value.bind="selectedCourses" multiple>
  <option repeat.for="course of courses"
   model.bind="course.id">${course.name}
  </option>
  </select>
 </label>
 Selected courses: ${selectedCourses}
 </form>
</template>
```

Computed properties

Let's say you just finished writing your security component to allow users to sign into your application, and you want to display their first and last names as a greeting in the header area of your screen. You can do this by creating a `computed` property even though the underlying data object does not expose this property. Computed properties allow you to combine multiple properties from a given object and expose them for binding on your view-model. Let's take a look at a simplified version of the welcome.js file:

Code Listing 87

```
export class Welcome {

  heading = 'Welcome to the Aurelia Navigation App!';

  firstName = 'John';

  lastName = 'Doe';

  previousValue = this.fullName;


  get fullName() {

  return `${this.firstName} ${this.lastName}`;

  }

}
```

Here we see the use of the `fullName` computed property. It simply returns the `firstName` and `lastName` properties from the `Welcome` class as a template string.

 Note: It is not possible to observe getters, and they must be "dirty-checked," which is very expensive. However, it is possible to let Aurelia know the properties this computed property is dependent upon. You can do this by using the `@computedFrom` decorator.

Here is a more efficient, optimized version using the `@computedFrom` decorator on our computed property:

Code Listing 88

```
import {computedFrom} from 'aurelia-framework';


export class Welcome {

  heading = 'Welcome to the Aurelia Navigation App!';

  firstName = 'John';

  lastName = 'Doe';
```

```
previousValue = this.fullName;


@computedFrom('firstName', 'lastName')

get fullName() {

return `${this.firstName} ${this.lastName}`;

}

}
```

This provides a lot of flexibility when you want to bind to a single property, but still receive updates when the underlying dependent properties change.

Value converters

Value converters allow the developer to define data transformation during the binding process bubbling up from the view-model or modified by the user from the view. We can look again to the welcome.js file to see usage of a value converter:

Code Listing 89

```
import {computedFrom} from 'aurelia-framework';


export class Welcome {
  heading = 'Welcome to the Aurelia Navigation App!';
  firstName = 'John';
  lastName = 'Doe';
  previousValue = this.fullName;


  @computedFrom('firstName', 'lastName')
  get fullName() {
  return `${this.firstName} ${this.lastName}`;
  }
}


export class UpperValueConverter {
  toView(value) {
  return value && value.toUpperCase();
  }
}
```

In this simplified file, we see the class `UpperValueConverter`, and the `toView` function, which lets us know that we are converting the value from our view-model to the view. The other function available is the `fromView`, which, as the name suggests, takes the value from the view and updates the view-model.

Let's take a look at how we use this newly created value converter in our simplified welcome.html file:

Code Listing 90

```
<template>
```

```
<section class="au-animate">
<form role="form">
 <div class="form-group">
 <label>Full Name</label>
 <p class="help-block">${fullName | upper}</p>
 </div>
</form>
</section>
</template>
```

As you can see, we are using the value converter when we are interpolating the **fullName** property inside the paragraph element. The syntax is: `${<property> | <value-converter>}`.

 Note: We are able to reference the UpperValueConverter *as "upper" since Aurelia has a default convention of looking for a class that has the name* Upper *with a suffix,* ValueConverter*, attached to it.*

There is so much more you can do with value converters; look here for more examples.

Binding behaviors

If you need something more powerful than a value converter, then binding behaviors are exactly what you are looking for. Binding behaviors give you full access to a binding throughout its lifecycle. This differs from value converters in that they only have access to the value bubbling up from the view-model or modified by the user on the view. This added power gives binding behaviors the opportunity to change the behavior of the binding.

There are a couple of rules that you need to be aware of when dealing with binding behaviors:

- A binding behavior can accept arguments using the colon (:) as the delimiter.
- A binding expression can be comprised of multiple binding behaviors.
- A binding expression can be comprised of multiple value converters and binding behaviors. The value converters must always come first.

Let's define a use case and see if we might be able to use a binding behavior to satisfy the requirement. You are tasked with creating a screen where users will type into an input element to search, and after the user has finished typing, the screen will perform a lookup via a Web API call to a back end for querying the results. Let's take a look at the following example to see how this might be accomplished:

Code Listing 91

```
<template>
 <form role="form">
 <div class="form-group">
  <label>Search:</label>
  <input type="text" value.bind="criteria & debounce"
  change.delegate="performSearch()">
 </div>
 </form>
</template>
```

You will notice in our `value.bind` expression that we are introducing the ampersand (`&`) character. It is this character that identifies that we are going to be passing in a binding behavior. In our case, it will be `debounce`. The `debounce` binding behavior allows users to type into an input, but it will not update the underlying property that it is bound to until 200 milliseconds have passed. This is very similar to the value converter pipe (|) notation that we looked at earlier. The difference here is that we are not changing the underlying value in the binding, but adding a specific behavior.

In this case, we do not want the `change` event to fire with every keystroke the user makes, but after a brief period. This is where binding behaviors become powerful.

We can override the default time as follows:

Code Listing 92

```
<template>
 <form role="form">
 <div class="form-group">
  <label>Search:</label>
  <input type="text" value.bind="criteria & debounce:500"
  change.delegate="performSearch()">
 </div>
 </form>
</template>
```

Here, we are stating that we don't want an update to fire until 500 milliseconds have passed from the last change the user entered. This is exactly what we want, and prevents our function `performSearch` from being called too many times.

The following is a short list of the binding behaviors Aurelia has out of the box:

- `throttle`–Limits the rate at which the view-model is updated in two-way binding scenarios, or limits the rate at which the view is updated in one-way binding scenarios.
- `debounce`–Prevents the binding from being updated until a specified time has passed without any changes.
- `updateTrigger`–Gives the ability to override the input events that cause the element's value to be updated on the view-model. The default events are `change` and `input`.
- `signal`–This allows for signaling a change to other parts of your screen that are not aware of the change. A common example would be to allow a user to switch the language in which they are viewing your screen.
- `oneTime`–This comes in handy for string interpolation expressions. We already have this capability in our binding expression. Simply put, it will allow for the expression to be evaluated once and then remain the same regardless of any subsequent changes on the view-model.

Please refer here for further discussion on each of these powerful binding behaviors.

You have seen what Aurelia brings to the table, but what if you have a scenario that requires something unique? No worries—you can create your own custom binding behavior. The syntax for creating a custom binding behavior is very similar to a value converter. You are provided with two methods: `bind(binding, scope, [...args])` and `unbind(binding, scope)`. In the `bind` method, you apply your behavior to the binding; in the `unbind` method, you clean up anything you did to the binding and restore it back to its original state.

Please refer here for further discussion on creating your own binding behavior. We will go over creating our own custom binding behavior in Chapter 10.

Chapter 6 Routing

Overview

Navigating through your application is a crucial part of a user experience, and Aurelia comes ready with a very powerful router. It takes a single Aurelia element to get your application ready to use the router. Let's look at what is required to get your router set up:

Code Listing 93

```
<template>
 <router-view></router-view>
</template>
```

We see that we are using the `router-view` element. It performs all the heavy lifting with regard to responding when a route has changed. If you recall, we reviewed the `configureRouter` method in Chapter 4. If we examine the `config.map` function, we see that it takes in an array of `RouteConfig` objects. Each `RouteConfig` object represents a given route. Here are all the properties that make up the `RouteConfig` object:

- `route`–The route pattern to match against incoming URL fragments, or an array of patterns.
- `name`–A unique name for the route that may be used to identify when generating URL fragments.
- `moduleId`–The module ID of the view-model that should be activated for this route.
- `redirect`–A URL fragment to redirect to when this route is matched.
- `navigationStrategy`–A function that can be used to dynamically select the module or modules to activate. The function is passed the current `NavigationInstruction`, and should configure `instruction.config` with the desired `moduleId`, `viewPorts`, or `redirect`.
- `viewPorts`–The view ports to target when activating this route. If unspecified, the target module ID is loaded into the default viewport (the viewport with name `default`). The `viewPorts` object should have keys whose property names correspond to names used by `<router-view>` elements. The values should be objects specifying the module ID to load into that view port.
- `nav`–When specified, this route will be included in the `Router.navigation` nav model. Useful for dynamically generating menus or other navigation elements. When a number is specified, that value will be used as a sort order.

- `href`–The URL fragment to use in `nav` models. If unspecified, the `RouteConfig.route` will be used. However, if the `RouteConfig.route` contains dynamic segments, this property must be specified.
- `generationUsesHref`–Indicates that when route generation is done for this route, it should just take the literal value of the `href` property.
- `title`–The document title to set when this route is active.
- `settings`–Arbitrary data to attach to the route. This can be used to attach custom data needed by components like pipeline steps and activated modules.
- `navModel`–The navigation model for storing and interacting with the route's navigation settings.
- `caseSensitive`–When `true` is specified, this route will be case sensitive.
- `activationStrategy`–Add to specify an activation strategy if it is always the same and you do not want that to be in your view-model code. Available values are `replace` and `invoke-lifecycle`.

As you can see from the properties, you have a lot of power with how you want to configure your routes. Let's look at a typical configuration:

Code Listing 94

```
export class App {
 configureRouter(config, router) {
 config.title = 'Aurelia';
 config.map([
  {
  route: ['', 'home'],
  name: 'home',
  moduleId: './home',
  nav: true,
  title: 'Home'
  },
  {
  route: 'blogs',
  name: 'blogs',
  moduleId: './blogs',
  nav: true,
  title: 'Blogs'
```

```
    },
    {
    route: 'blogs/:id',

    name: 'blog-detail',

    moduleId: './blog-detail',

    nav: false,

    title: 'Blog Detail'

    }
  ]);


  this.router = router;

  }

}
```

In this example, we have defined three routes. The first route is our default route due to the presence of the empty string (`''`) as part of the match patterns for the `route` property. Also notice that we have identified a *parameterized route* for the `blog-detail`. The convention is a colon (`:`) followed by the name of the parameter. Besides parameterized routes, you can also specify *wildcard routes* using the asterisk (`*`) followed by the name of the parameter to represent the rest of the path. You will also need to provide an `href` entry in the route when you do this.

The `moduleId` is where Aurelia looks to find the view-model for activation. This can represent any folder structure if you wish to organize your view-models in a certain way. This is common in feature-driven folder structures. Note that we are not using the `nav` property for every route. By setting `nav` to `false` or omitting the property, we are specifying that we do not wish it to be part of the router navigation nav model that is used when generating our menus. Finally, `title` is what will be displayed in our menus from the router navigation nav model.

Pipelines

Sometimes it is necessary to perform business logic before or after we navigate to a given route. That is what pipelines bring to the table, and following is a breakdown of each:

- `authorize`–Called between loading the route's step and calling the route view-model's `canActivate` function, if defined.
- `preActivate`–Called between the route view-model's `canActivate` function and the previous route view-model's `deactivate` function, if defined.
- `preRender`–Called between the route view-model's `activate` function and before the component is rendered or composed.
- `postRender`–Called after the component has been rendered or composed.

So, if we would like to create an authorize step and add it to the pipeline, we would do something like the following:

Code Listing 95

```
import AuthorizeStep from './authorize-step';


export class App {
 configureRouter(config, router) {
 config.title = 'Aurelia';
 config.addPipelineStep('authorize', AuthorizeStep);
 config.map([
  { route: 'home', moduleId: './home', title: 'Home',
  settings: { roles: [] } },
  { route: 'blogs', moduleId: './blogs', title: 'Blogs',
  settings: { roles: ['admin'] },
  { route: 'blog/:id', moduleId: './blog-detail',
  title: 'Blog Detail', settings: { roles: ['admin'] } }
 ]);


 this.router = router;
 }
}
```

As you can see, we are importing the `AuthorizeStep` so that we can use it when we call the `addPipelineStep` function. Also notice that we are using the `settings` property and passing in some custom data that we will look for in the `AuthorizeStep` class.

 Note: Make sure that you use the correct spelling when you pass in the first argument to the `addPipelineStep`.

Let's now look at the `AuthorizeStep` class:

Code Listing 96

```
export class AuthorizeStep {
 run(navigationInstruction, next) {
  if (navigationInstruction.getAllInstructions()
   .some(i => i.config.settings.roles.indexOf('admin') !== -1)) {
   var isAdmin = /* insert logic to determine if user is admin here */ false;
   if (!isAdmin) {
    return next.cancel(new Redirect('home'));
   }
  }


  return next();
 }
}
```

This is a very simple example, but I hope it gives you an idea of what you can do. We are interrogating the `settings` property of each of the routes and checking to see if the `roles` array contains a value of `admin`. If it does find a match, then we have a variable that would represent whether or not the current user is an admin or not. If the `isAdmin` is `false`, then we ignore the routing instruction and redirect back to the home screen.

If you'd like to learn more, please refer here.

Screen lifecycle

As we saw from the pipelines, there are certain points in a screen lifecycle that we can tap into. Aurelia provides screens with the ability to influence the activation lifecycle. Let's look at the hooks provided:

- `canActivate(params, routeConfig, navigationInstruction)` –This hook allows you to control whether or not your view-model can be navigated to. You can return a Boolean value, a promise for a Boolean value, or a `navigation` command.

- `activate(params, routeConfig, navigationInstruction)` –This hook allows you to perform custom logic before your view-model is displayed. You can optionally return a promise so that the router will wait to bind and attach the view until your promise returns.

- `canDeactivate()` –This hook allows you to control whether or not the router can navigate away from your view-model. You can return a Boolean value, a promise for a Boolean value, or a `navigation` command.

- `deactivate()` –This hook allows you to perform custom logic when your view-model is being navigated away from. You can optionally return a promise so that the router will wait until after the promise returns.

Each of these hooks is powerful and you will find a lot of value as you start to use them. A common example would be using the `canDeactivate` hook to ensure that the user isn't trying to navigate away from a dirty screen, meaning they need to save their changes or finish an important action before they can navigate away from the screen.

Chapter 7 Components

Overview

Components are the basic building blocks in Aurelia. You will find that components are the screens and custom elements that you create. If you think about it, the screens that we create are a form of a custom element. Components are comprised of two files: view and view-model. Because Aurelia understands how to work with components, it is able to provide a robust lifecycle ensuring consistency and stability. This is achieved through the templating engine and dependency injection. Once a component has been instantiated, Aurelia is able to link the view and view-model together via databinding.

Component lifecycle

Every component has a consistent and predictable lifecycle. This gives us the ability to follow the lifecycle of the component. Let's look at each phase a component goes through:

1. `constructor`–This is the first function called on the view-model.
2. `created(owningView, myView)`–This function is called next if the view-model implements it. At this point in the lifecycle, the view has been created and both the view and view-model are connected to their controller. The `owningView` is the view where the component is declared. If this component has a view, it will be passed as `myView`.
3. `bind(bindingContext, overrideContext)`–This function is called next if the view-model implements it. At this point, databinding has been activated on the view and view-model. The `bindingContext` is the context to which this component is bound. The `overrideContext` contains information used to traverse the parent hierarchy, and is also used to add any contextual properties the component wants to add.
4. `attached()`–This function is called next if the view-model implements it. The component is now attached to the DOM.
5. `detached()`–When the component is removed from the DOM in the future, this function will be called if the view-model implements it.
6. `unbind()`–After the component is detached, this function will be called if the view-model implements it.

Every one of the hooks is optional. The latter four tend to go hand-in-hand—if you implement `bind`, then you would most likely implement `unbind` to clean up; likewise, if you implement `attached`, then you would most likely implement `detached` to clean up.

Chapter 8 Custom Elements

Overview

Custom elements are by far some of the most exciting pieces within Aurelia. You have the ability to create reusable components that can be as simple or as complicated as necessary. Suppose you would like to create a component that encapsulates the logic for an input element along with a label. Let's look at what it takes to create our first custom element. We will call it **my-input**. Let's look at the my-input.html file first:

Code Listing 97

```
<template>
  <label>${label}</label>
  <input type.bind="type"
    placeholder.bind="placeholder"
    value.bind="value">
</template>
```

In this example, we can see that we need four properties on our view-model: `label`, `type`, `placeholder`, and `value`. Let's now take a look at our my-input.js file:

Code Listing 98

```
import {customElement, bindable} from 'aurelia-framework';


@customElement('my-input')
export class MyInput {
  @bindable type = 'text';
  @bindable label;
  @bindable placeholder = '';
  @bindable value;


  constructor() {
  }
```

}

We create our file and it then defines a custom element. We are exposing four attributes for this custom element that we are allowing the developer to bind to when using.

Let's see what it takes to use our new custom element in a screen:

Code Listing 99

```
<template>
  <require from='my-input'></require>
  <h1>${title}</h1>
  <form>
  <my-input label="Customer Name"
   placeholder="Enter your name..."
   value.two-way="customerName"></my-input>
  <p>${customerName}</p>
  </form>
</template>
```

As you can see, that is pretty slick. We have reduced a ton of markup, yet still have a very simple API. Also notice that we did not provide a type. We don't have to if we want the type to remain `text`. We only have to provide a type if we wish to override the default value. Here is a screenshot of this example:

Figure 27: Custom Element–my-input

You can see this example in action here.

Content projection

There will be times when you are authoring a custom element for which you want to allow a developer who uses your element to inject content. Say we want to create a panel element where we will have a header and body section to the element. In the header, we will just bind to a heading, but we want to allow the developer to provide any content into the body. Let's look at the following bs-panel.html file:

Code Listing 100

```
<template>
 <div class="panel">
 <div class="panel-heading">
  ${header}
 </div>
 <div class="panel-body">
  <slot></slot>
 </div>
 </div>
</template>
```

Let's take a look at the bs-panel.js file:

Code Listing 101

```
import {customElement, bindable} from 'aurelia-framework';


@customElement('bs-panel')
export class BsPanel {
 @bindable header = '';


 constructor() {


 }
}
```

Now let's take a look at how we use our new custom element:

Code Listing 102

```
<template>

 <require from='bs-panel'></require>

 <h1>${title}</h1>

 <bs-panel header="My Discourse">

 <p>Four score and seven years ago...</p>

 </bs-panel>

</template>
```

As you can see, you are able to put in any content you like. You don't even have to change your programming paradigm, as the content just works. Let's see what this looks like:

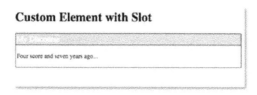

Figure 28: Custom element with slot

You can see this example in action here.

Chapter 9 Custom Attributes

Overview

Sometimes we don't need to create a whole new custom element, but just need to extend the functionality of an existing element. Perhaps we want to have the behavior of the attribute to be to focus on whichever element we choose when we navigate the first time to our screen. We will call our custom attribute `my-focus`. Let's take a look at the my-focus.js file:

Code Listing 103

```
import {customAttribute, DOM} from 'aurelia-templating';


@customAttribute('my-focus')
export class MyFocus {
  static inject = [DOM.Element];

  constructor(element) {
  this.element = element;
  }

  attached() {
  this.element.focus();
  }
}
```

Here, we are identifying our class as a custom attribute. We are also injecting the DOM element to which this attribute is attached. This gives us the ability to access properties or call methods off of the object like we are doing when our custom attribute is attached to the element.

This seems straightforward enough; now let's see how we actually use this in a screen:

Code Listing 104

```
<template>
  <require from='my-focus'></require>
```

```
<h1>${title}</h1>
<form>
<label>First Name</label>
<input value.bind="firstName"
  placeholder="First Name" my-focus>
<p>${firstName}</p>
</form>
</template>
```

Here we are extending the input element so that when this screen loads and the `my-focus` custom attribute is attached, the `focus` method will be called.

 Note: The my-focus custom attribute makes the assumption that you will only attach it to one element for a given screen. Not all custom attributes will need to have this limitation, but that just depends on what logic you provide in our custom attributes.

As you can see, creating your own custom attributes is very straightforward, and you will find that you will have a suite of powerful additions to your toolbox.

Here is a screenshot of the custom attribute in action:

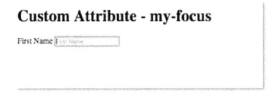

Figure 29: Custom Attribute–my-focus

You can see this example in action here.

Chapter 10 Custom Binding Behaviors

In Chapter 5, we were looking at the available binding behaviors packaged with Aurelia. In this chapter, we will look into what it takes to build our own custom binding behavior. As you recall, binding behaviors are the most similar to value converters. You use the ampersand (&) character to denote that we will be using a binding behavior. Binding behaviors give us a lot more access to the binding than simply converting values like the value converter does.

Let's consider the following use case. You are tasked with creating a registration screen that allows the user to choose a username. The system requires that this username be unique, so you must ensure that you perform a lookup as the user types. We will use the `debounce` binding behavior to help ensure that our custom binding behavior does not fire too many times. Let's take a look at how this can be accomplished:

Code Listing 105

```
const interceptMethods = ['updateTarget', 'updateSource', 'callSour
ce'];


export class UniqueBindingBehavior {
 bind(binding, scope, uniqueFunc) {
 let i = interceptMethods.length;
 while (i--) {
  let method = interceptMethods[i];
  if (!binding[method]) {
  continue;
  }
  binding[`intercepted-${method}`] = binding[method];
  let update = binding[method].bind(binding);
  binding[method] = uniqueFunc.bind(binding, method, update);
 }
 }


 unbind(binding, scope) {
 let i = interceptMethods.length;
```

```
while (i--) {
  let method = interceptMethods[i];
  if (!binding[method]) {
    continue;
  }
  binding[method] = binding[`intercepted-${method}`];
  binding[`intercepted-${method}`] = null;
  }
  }
}
```

This custom binding behavior will simply try to execute the `uniqueFunc` reference that it has whenever the binding receives an `updateTarget`, `updateSource`, or `callSource` notification.

The `uniqueFunc` must have the following signature: `(method, update, value)`. Let's look at how this is wired in markup:

Code Listing 106

```
<template>
  <require from='unique-binding-behavior'></require>
  <h1>${title}</h1>
  <form>
  <label>User Name</label>
  <input value.bind="username & unique:uniqueFunc & debounce:800">
  <p class="help-text">${lookupResult}</p>
  </form>
</template>
```

In this snippet, we actually have two binding behaviors. One is the `debounce` behavior that we get for free from Aurelia. We are stating that we don't want to update the `firstName` property on the view-model until 800 milliseconds have passed since the user has pressed a key. We also are using our unique custom binding behavior. It has a single argument that is a reference to the `uniqueFunc` function on the view-model. You will also notice that we also have a `paragraph` element that displays the value of the `lookupResult` property.

Let's now look at our view-model and see what we are doing here:

Code Listing 107

```
export class App {
  username = '';
  uniqueNames = ['matt', 'kevin', 'larry'];
  lookupResult = '';
  uniqueFunc;

  constructor() {
  this.uniqueFunc = (method, update, value) => {
    if (this.uniqueNames.includes(value)) {
     this.lookupResult = 'Sorry this username has already been used.';
    }
    else {
     this.lookupResult = '';
    }
    update(value);
  };
  }
}
```

As you can see from our view-model, we have a simple array, `uniqueName`, representing a list of names already in use. I use an array with fixed values for simplicity; in a real application, you'd have to update the array values as names are added. We have our `lookupResult` to allow us to display a message back to the user if the username that is typed has already been used. Finally, in our constructor, we have our `uniqueFunc` logic that simply checks to make sure the value typed is unique.

Here is a screenshot of the custom binding behavior in action:

Figure 30: UniqueBindingBehavior

You can look at this example here.

This is handy, but it still required a lot of code in our view-model to accomplish. What if we wanted to have the custom binding behavior handle the bulk of the logic? Let's take a stab at reworking our binding behavior to do just that. Consider the following:

Code Listing 108

```
const interceptMethods = ['updateTarget', 'updateSource', 'callSour
ce'];


export class UniqueBindingBehavior {

 uniqueFunc(method, update, $this, uniqueArray, resultHandler, valu
e) {

 if (uniqueArray.includes(value)) {

  $this[resultHandler] = 'Sorry this username has already been used
.';

 }

 else {

  $this[resultHandler] = '';

 }

 update(value);

 }


 bind(binding, scope, $this, uniqueArray, resultHandler) {

 let i = interceptMethods.length;

 while (i--) {

  let method = interceptMethods[i];

  if (!binding[method]) {

  continue;

  }

  binding[`intercepted-${method}`] = binding[method];

  let update = binding[method].bind(binding);

  binding[method] = this.uniqueFunc.bind(binding, method,

  update, $this, uniqueArray, resultHandler);
```

```
    }
  }

  unbind(binding, scope) {
  let i = interceptMethods.length;
  while (i--) {
    let method = interceptMethods[i];
    if (!binding[method]) {
    continue;
    }
    binding[method] = binding[`intercepted-${method}`];
    binding[`intercepted-${method}`] = null;
  }
  }
}
```

This time, we have placed the logic of determining the uniqueness of the username into the custom binding behavior. It is flexible enough to receive any array. It also has a generic `resultHandler` that allows you to update the view-model once uniqueness has been determined. Our custom binding behavior now is expecting three arguments: `$this`, `uniqueArray`, and `resultHandler`. We need a handle to the view-model, `$this`, so that we can use the string representation held in the `resultHandler` property to update the view-model. Finally, we also expect an array that will check the uniqueness of the value entered.

Here's how the markup would look for this:

Code Listing 109

```
<template>
  <require from='unique-binding-behavior'></require>
  <h1>${title}</h1>
  <form>
  <label>User Name</label>
  <input value.bind="username & unique:$this:uniqueNames:'lookupResu
lt' & debounce:800">
  <p class="help-text">${lookupResult}</p>
```

```
  </form>
</template>
```

Our custom binding behavior uses the `$this` keyword that we get for free from Aurelia to reference our view-model. Next, we are passing in a reference to the `uniqueNames` array. Finally, we pass a string representing the `lookupResult` property so that we can update the view-model from the custom binding behavior. The change that we need to make to our view-model is simply to remove the `uniqueFunc` function, as it is no longer necessary.

You can see this example in action here.

Please refer here for more information on custom binding behaviors.

Chapter 11 Services

Overview

In this chapter, we will go over authoring services for encapsulating business logic that can be shared across all view-models via dependency injection. We will also discuss HTTP Services, focusing on the `aurelia-fetch-client`. Let's start with discussing services in general.

General services

Services are a great way to encapsulate logic and data that may need to be referenced in multiple places in your application and across multiple classes. We will introduce a simple service called **AppService**. The **AppService** is a general-purpose property bag that will allow us to have common data in one place across our application. We will be able to inject this service into any view-model that desires to have access to properties and methods on this class. For our purposes, we will just have a simple API. Let's take a look at the file *app-service.js*:

Code Listing 110

```
export class AppService {
  user;


  constructor() {


  }
}
```

This simple class allows us to assign a user object to the **AppService** class, and then share it with any other view-model that desires access to the current user.

We use this service in our order-history.js file, as shown in the following code:

Code Listing 111

```
imports {AppService} from './services/app-service';
imports {DataService} from './services/data-service';


export class OrderHistory {
  static inject = [AppService, DataService];


  constructor(appService, dataService) {
  this.appService = appService;
  this.dataService = dataService;
  }


  async activate() {
```

```
  this.data = await this.dataService.getOrdersByUserId(
    this.appService.user.id);
  }


}
```

In this example, we are bringing in two dependencies: `AppService` and `DataService`. We need the `AppService` so that we can make a call in our `DataService` to get `Orders` for a given user by their ID. By using the `AppService` singleton, we are able to attach application-level data to the object and inject it into any of the screens and services that need it.

DataService

Besides generic services, let's focus our attention on HTTP Services and see how we might be able to access data. With that said, Aurelia comes with two services available:

- `aurelia-http-client`—This is a basic `HTTPClient` based on `XMLHttpRequest`. It supports all HTTP verbs, JSONP (to bypass cross-domain policies), and request cancellation.
- `aurelia-fetch-client`—This is an `HTTPClient` based on the `Fetch` specification. It supports all HTTP verbs and integrates with service workers, including request/response caching.

We will be using the `aurelia-fetch-client` for our example. Please refer to the Aurelia documentation here to better help you make the right decision about which one to use.

We are now ready to take a look at what the `DataService` class might look like. Consider the following:

Code Listing 112

```
import {HttpClient} from 'aurelia-fetch-client';


// polyfill fetch client conditionally
const fetch = !self.fetch ? System.import('isomorphic-fetch') :
 Promise.resolve(self.fetch);


export class DataService {
 static inject = [HttpClient];


 constructor(http) {
 http.configure(config => {
  config
  .useStandardConfiguration()
  .withBaseUrl('<add your base URL here>');
 });
 this.http = http;
 }
```

```
async getOrdersByUserId(userId) {
try {
 let response = await this.http.fetch(`orders/${userId}`);
 let data = await response.json();
 return data;
} catch(error) {
 console.log(error);
 return null;
 }
 }
}
```

After we import **aurelia-fetch-client**, we are ensuring that the browser we are running under supports the **Fetch API**. Otherwise, we are bringing in a polyfill. Next, we are injecting the dependency into the constructor where we configure the service. We are using a standard configuration and leaving the base URL to be relative to whatever backend service you wish to call. Finally, we have our **getOrdersByUserId** function that takes in a **userId** as a parameter. This function is marked as **async**, and we see we are using the **await** keywords inside the method for any asynchronous operations. We finish by returning the data or by returning **null**, depending on if we encountered an exception or not.

The hardest part is done, and you should be able to extend this service out to handle **POST**, **PUT**, and **DELETE** verbs to make your **DataService** complete.

Chapter 12 Event Aggregation

We have looked at services and how they can come in handy, but what about times when we need to communicate events across classes? It would be really cool if Aurelia supported some form of publish/subscribe model in the framework. Well, look no further—that is exactly what the `aurelia-event-aggregator` does.

Consider the use case where you present a user with a login screen, and upon a successful login, you want to build up their dashboard and menu tree. This is all possible using the event aggregator. Let's take a look at an example:

Code Listing 113

```
imports {EventAggregator} from 'aurelia-framework';

imports {DataService} from './services/data-service';


export class Login {
  static inject = [EventAggregator, DataService];


  username = '';
  password = '';


  constructor(eventAggregator, dataService) {
  this.eventAggregator = eventAggregator;
  this.dataService = dataService;
  }


  async performLogin() {
  let response = await this.dataService.authenticate(
   this.username, this.password);
  if (response.success) {
   this.loginSuccess(response.user);
  }


  loginSuccess(user) {
```

```
this.eventAggregator.publish('login-success', user);

  }


}
```

We have our `Login` class, and we first call our `performLogin` function, which tries to authenticate our user by passing in `username` and `password`. It returns a `response` object that has a Boolean `success` property as well as a `user` property, if successful. If the user passes authentication, then we call `loginSuccess`, passing in the `user` object. The event aggregator publishes a channel with the name `login-success` and the payload of the user object.

It is important to have a good handle on your channels that you use with the event aggregator. A common approach might be to create a `ChannelService` that simply has all of the channels that your application uses for communication over the event aggregator. This will help mitigate any potential problems with misspellings, etc. It is also possible to use types in the form of a class to represent the channel.

Let's take a look at how we might subscribe to this event. Consider the following:

Code Listing 114

```
imports {EventAggregator} from 'aurelia-framework';
imports {DataService} from './services/data-service';


export class Welcome {
  static inject = [EventAggregator, DataService];


  dashboard = [];


  constructor(eventAggregator, dataService) {
  this.eventAggregator = eventAggregator;
  this.dataService = dataService;


  this.eventAggregator.subscribe('login-success',
    this.onLoginSuccess);
  }
```

```
onLoginSuccess(user) {

this.dashboard = await this.dataService.getDashboardByUserId(

 user.id);

 }


}
```

Here we are subscribing to the `login-success` channel. We pass the `onLoginSuccess` callback, and it in turn performs a lookup to get dashboard information based on the user ID. The event aggregator gives us the ability to provide rich communication across our classes, and yet still preserve separation of concerns.

Chapter 13 Compose

When designing an effective user experience, you may need to choose a certain component based on data on the screen. For example, let's say we are building an operations monitoring screen. One of the facets of the screen is that we would like to have a different view displayed based on individual data items. We will simply make several views and have them show based on a specific data property. The following is a simple screenshot of what we are going to build using `compose`:

Figure 31: Using compose

In Figure 31, we have an array that holds server information. We then use the `compose` element to target which view-model to load for a given server. Let's look at our operations-monitor.js file:

Code Listing 115

```
export class OperationsMonitor {
 title = 'Operations Servers Dashboard'
 servers = [
 { name: 'hemlock', status: 'red',
  message: 'System down',
  error: 'Hurricane Bob has taken out the eastern seaboard!' },
 { name: 'birch', status: 'green',
  message: 'Birch is all thumbs up!' },
 { name: 'laurel', status: 'orange',
```

```
  message: 'Something\'s fishy going on...',
  warning: 'Check to see if it is plugged in!' },
{ name: 'willow', status: 'green',
  message: 'Willow is healthy!' },
];


}
```

You should start to see the pattern emerging just by looking at the code alone. Let's look at the corresponding operations-monitor.html file:

Code Listing 116

```
<template>
 <h1>${title}</h1>
 <compose repeat.for="server of servers"
 view-model.bind="server.status" model.bind="server"></compose>
</template>
```

We see now that we are repeating over every item in the **servers** array. We are binding our view-model to the **status** property of each server, and we are also setting the **model** context to the **server** object.

Following the convention Aurelia has set up, we should be able to deduce that the first item in the array has a status of **red**. Aurelia will try to look up a corresponding red.js view-model. In turn, red.html will also load. Let's look at red.js:

Code Listing 117

```
export class Red {


}
```

As you can see, we don't have any custom business logic. Let's now look at red.html:

Code Listing 118

```
<template>
 <div class="server ${server.status}">
 <h1>${server.name}</h1>
 <h3>${server.message}</h3>
 <p>${server.error}</p>
```

```
  </div>
</template>
```

As you can see, we are binding specific information for the red status. If we were to look at the green and orange view-model files, they would be exactly the same. However, let's look at the difference in the views. Let's look at the orange.html file:

Code Listing 119

```
<template>
  <div class="server ${server.status}">
  <h1>${server.name}</h1>
  <h3>${server.message}</h3>
  <p>${server.warning}</p>
  </div>
</template>
```

As you can see, the only difference here is we are binding to warning instead of error. Let's look at the green.html view:

Code Listing 120

```
<template>
  <div class="server ${server.status}">
  <h1>${server.name}</h1>
  <h3>${server.message}</h3>
  </div>
</template>
```

Again, this one is slightly different. You should have an idea as to how you could use this, and the different kinds of dynamic scenarios you could solve using the `compose` element.

Although this is a contrived example, it does show what you can do and the power it affords to building rich applications. If you are curious about the styles used in this example, the following is the CSS we used:

Code Listing 121

```
.server {
  color: white;
  height: 150px;
```

```css
  padding: 15px;
  margin: 15px;
  border-radius: 15px;
}
.red {
  background: red;
  width: 90%;
}
.green {
  background: green;
}
.orange {
  background: orange;
}
.green, .orange {
  width: 41%;
  float: left;
}
```

You can see this example in action here.

Chapter 14 Dynamic Views

We have seen how we can use Aurelia's compose capabilities for dynamic scenarios to handle bits and pieces of our screen. What about scenarios where we want to have the whole screen be dynamic? We could use `compose` again, but what if we wanted our screen markup to come from a database? This is where `getViewStrategy` comes in. It gives us the ability to pass in a string that represents our view. Let's take a look at our dynamic.js file:

Code Listing 122

```
import {InlineViewStrategy} from 'aurelia-templating';


export class Dynamic {


  constructor() {
  }


  getViewStrategy() {
  let template = `
   <template>
   <h2>Inside dynamic template!</h2>
   </template>
  `;
  let vs = new InlineViewStrategy(template, this);
  return vs;

  }

}
```

In all of your view-models, Aurelia provides the ability to change the default convention for how views and view-models are loaded. Here, we are hijacking the view strategy process and providing our own implementation. We use the `InlineViewStrategy` to allow us to provide our template. Aurelia doesn't care where we get the template, so it could be inline like we have here, or from a data service call.

In this example, we used a `compose` element to point to our view-model. You can see how we did this in the following app.html file:

Code Listing 123

```
<template>
 <h1>${title}</h1>
 <compose view-model="dynamic"></compose>
</template>
```

Here is the app.js file:

Code Listing 124

```
export class App {
 title = 'Dynamic Screens'
}
```

The following is a screenshot of what you should see:

Dynamic Screens

Inside dynamic template!

Figure 32: Dynamic template

You can see this example in action here.

Let's mix things up bit and introduce a view service so that we can simulate getting our views from a back-end server. Consider the following view-service.js file:

Code Listing 125

```
/**
 * Provides view markup.
 *
 * @class ViewService
 */
export class ViewService {

 constructor() {
```

```
    this.views = [];
    this.initViews();
    }


    getView(name) {
    return this.views.find((v) => {
      return v.name === name;
    })
    }


    initViews() {
    this.views = [
      {
      name: 'simple',
      view: `
        <template>
        <h2>Inside simple dynamic template!</h2>
        </template>

      `

      }
    ];
    }
}
```

Currently, this view service only has one **view** definition, but we will add another soon. The service has a **views** array that contains all of our view definitions. We have a helper **getView** function that allows us to pass in the name of the view and return the item found. We also have an **initViews** function that sets up all our views. This represents what we received back from a data service call.

Let's see how our dynamic.js file would look now that we have a view service created:

Code Listing 126

```
import {InlineViewStrategy} from 'aurelia-templating';
```

```
import {ViewService} from './view-service';


export class Dynamic {
  static inject = [ViewService];


  constructor(viewService) {
    this.viewService = viewService;
  }


  getViewStrategy() {
    let template = this.viewService.getView('simple');
    let vs = new InlineViewStrategy(template.view, this);
    return vs;
  }
}
```

Here, we are importing our `ViewService` and injecting it into our constructor. In our `getViewStrategy` function, we call the `getView` function, passing in `simple` for the name of the view.

You can see this example in action here.

Let's go a step further and add another view to our view service file, this time with some databinding:

Code Listing 127

```
/**
 * Provides view markup.
 *
 * @class ViewService
 */
export class ViewService {

  constructor() {
    this.views = [];
    this.initViews();
```

```javascript
}

getView(name) {
return this.views.find((v) => {
 return v.name === name;
})
}

initViews() {
this.views = [
 {
 name: 'simple',
 view: `
  <template>
  <h2>Inside simple dynamic template!</h2>
  </template>

 `
 },
 {
 name: 'data-entry',
 model: {
  heading: 'User Registration',
  username: ''
 },
 handlers: {
  submit: (payload) => {
  alert(`Saving ${payload}`);
  },
  cancel: (payload) => {
  alert('canceling');
  }
 },
```

```
view: `

  <template>

  <form role="form"

    submit.delegate="controller.handlers.submit(controller.model.us
ername)">

    <h1>\${controller.model.heading}</h1>

    <label for="username">Username</label>

    <input type="text"

     value.bind="controller.model.username"

     id="username"

     placeholder="User Name">

    <button type="submit">

     Submit

    </button>

    <button type="button"

     click.delegate="controller.handlers.cancel()">

     Cancel

    </button>

  </form>

  </template>

  `

  }

 ];

 }

}
```

We have now added a **data-entry** view definition. We see that we have a simple
user registration form. We are binding the **submit** event on the form. Notice that we
are referencing a **controller** variable on our view-model, which simply represents
this record in the view service. You will see that all of our bindings are attached to
either the **model** or **handlers** properties. This allows us to not only bring in a
dynamic view, but also dynamic logic that corresponds to the views.

> *Note: You may have noticed that we are escaping (\) the $ symbol for the heading. If we did not do*
> *this, the string interpolation would be executed immediately in our view-model, and we want to have*
> *this executed after our template has been loaded. Take note to do the same if you are using string*

interpolation in your dynamic templates.

Let's take a look at what we did to the dynamic.js file for this example:

Code Listing 128

```
import {InlineViewStrategy} from 'aurelia-templating';
import {ViewService} from './view-service';


export class Dynamic {
  static inject = [ViewService];


  controller;


  constructor(viewService) {
  this.viewService = viewService;
  }


  getViewStrategy() {
  let template = this.viewService.getView('data-entry');
  this.controller = template;
  let vs = new InlineViewStrategy(template.view, this);
  return vs;
  }
}
```

We load our new **data-entry** view by calling the **getView** function. Next, we set our **controller** property in the **getViewStrategy** function.

Let's see what this renders:

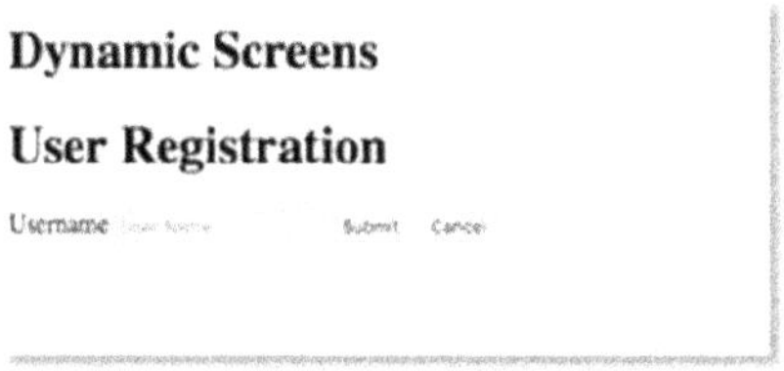

Dynamic Screens

User Registration

Username [   ]   Submit   Cancel

Figure 33: ViewService with databinding

Here is the screen when we put in a username and click **Submit**:

Figure 34: ViewService with click.delegate

You can see this example in action here.

Hopefully, this gives you an idea as to what you can do with `getViewStrategy` and service calls. Like all bright and shiny new toys, take care how you use this, but it does present a lot of interesting possibilities.

Chapter 15 Features

You might find that you have created a lot of custom elements, custom attributes, and custom binding behaviors, and you are getting tired of using the `require` tag in your HTML. Aurelia makes this very easy to do in the form of features. Typically, you will want to structure your components in a folder that allows for a clear separation from the rest of your application. A good example would be a folder called resources, and inside this folder, you would have your components like resources/my-components.

Going back to the `bs-input` and `attach-focus` components, we would have a file structure as follows:

Code Listing 129

```
root/
 src/
 resources/
  my-components/
  bs-input.html
  bs-input.js
  attach-focus.js
  index.js
 app.html
 app.js
 main.js
 index.html
 ...
```

So, if we use the following structure, we can define our feature by using the last file, index.js. Let's see what this would look like:

Code Listing 130

```
export function configure(config) {
 config.globalResources(
 './bs-input',
 './attach-focus',
 );
```

```
}
```

We are now finished with our structuring and organization. Let's now take the final step and bring in our feature. We do this in our main.js file as follows:

Code Listing 131

```
import '../styles/styles.css';

import 'font-awesome/css/font-awesome.css';

import 'bootstrap/dist/css/bootstrap.css';

import 'bootstrap';


import * as Bluebird from 'bluebird';

Bluebird.config({ warnings: false });


export async function configure(aurelia) {

  aurelia.use

  .standardConfiguration()

  .developmentLogging()

  .feature('resources/my-components');


  await aurelia.start();

  aurelia.setRoot('app');

}
```

That's all there is to it! You add a single line feature with the location of your components, and you get them everywhere in your application without needing to use the `require` tag.

Chapter 16 Plugins

Perhaps you are ready to take your components to the next level and allow other developers to use and reference them. You would accomplish this by creating a plugin so that any developer can use the package manager to install your components. As we have been using WebPack throughout this book, I will walk you through registering your plugin with Node Package Manager so that it can be installed on a developer's box.

Plugins require a little more work with the third-party package managers, but once in place, using a plugin is a breeze. One thing to consider is that you should ensure the names of your components are unique and do not conflict with an Aurelia component or another third party. A common approach to solving this is to provide a prefix in front of all of your components to help keep their names unique. Let's pretend that we are going to use the `bs` prefix and have the names `bs-input` and `bs-attach-focus` for our components.

We will want to have a separate project for our plugin repository. We will use GitHub for our repository. Let's take a look at what the package.json would look like in our new project:

Code Listing 132

```
{
  "name": "aurelia-succinctly",
  "version": "0.0.1",
  "description": "This is a set of components for the Aurelia Succin
ctly book.",
  "keywords": [
  "aurelia",
  "plugin"
  ],
  "homepage": "http://mattduffield.wordpress.com",
  "bugs": {
  "url": "https://github.com/mattduffield/aurelia-succinctly/issues"
  },
  "license": "CC0-1.0",
  "author": "Matt Duffield <matt.duffield@gmail.com> (http://mattduf
field.wordpress.com/)",
```

```
"main": "dist/commonjs/index.js",
"repository": {
"type": "git",
"url": "http://github.com/mattduffield/aurelia-succinctly"
},
"aurelia": {
"build": {
 "resources": [
 "aurelia-succinctly/bs-input",
 "aurelia-succinctly/bs-attach-focus"
 ]
}
},
"devDependencies": {
"aurelia-tools": "^0.2.4",
"babel": "^6.5.2",
"babel-eslint": "^6.1.2",
"babel-plugin-syntax-flow": "^6.8.0",
"babel-plugin-transform-decorators-legacy": "^1.3.4",
"babel-plugin-transform-es2015-modules-amd": "^6.8.0",
"babel-plugin-transform-es2015-modules-commonjs": "^6.11.5",
"babel-plugin-transform-es2015-modules-systemjs": "^6.11.6",
"babel-plugin-transform-flow-strip-types": "^6.8.0",
"babel-preset-es2015": "^6.9.0",
"babel-preset-es2015-loose": "^7.0.0",
"babel-preset-stage-1": "^6.5.0",
"conventional-changelog": "1.1.0",
"del": "^2.2.1",
"gulp": "^3.9.1",
"gulp-babel": "^6.1.2",
"gulp-bump": "^2.2.0",
"gulp-eslint": "^3.0.1",
```

```
"gulp-yuidoc": "^0.1.2",
"isparta": "^4.0.0",
"istanbul": "^1.0.0-alpha.2",
"jasmine-core": "^2.4.1",
"karma": "^1.1.2",
"karma-babel-preprocessor": "^6.0.1",
"karma-chrome-launcher": "^1.0.1",
"karma-coverage": "^1.1.1",
"karma-jasmine": "^1.0.2",
"karma-jspm": "2.2.0",
"object.assign": "^4.0.4",
"require-dir": "^0.3.0",
"run-sequence": "^1.2.2",
"vinyl-paths": "^2.1.0",
"yargs": "^4.8.1"
},
"jspm": {
"registry": "npm",
"jspmPackage": true,
"main": "index",
"format": "amd",
"directories": {
 "dist": "dist/amd"
},
"peerDependencies": {},
"devDependencies": {
 "aurelia-polyfills": "^1.0.0-beta.1.1.0"
}
}
}
```

Please provide your own pertinent information from **name** down to **repository**.
Under the section aurelia/build/resources, you will want to identify all of your

components you wish to publish. Finally, provide whatever `devDependencies` and `jspm` entries you like.

The file structure for your project should look like the following:

Code Listing 133

```
aurelia-succinctly/
 build/
 dist/
 doc/
 CHANGELOG.md
 node_modules/
 src/
 bs-input.html
 bs-input.js
 attach-focus.js
 index.js
 test/
 .gitignore
 config.js
 gulpfile.js
 karma.conf.js
 LICENSE
 package.json
 README.md
```

This structure follows what you would see in the Skeleton Navigation example, with the exception that you only have your components in the src/ folder. The build/ folder handles all the building and bundling of the source code. The dist/ folder is what you get when you bundle your source for ready for deployment. The *doc/* folder is where you would have your change log. The node_modules/ folder is what you get when you run `npm install`. The src/ folder is where all of your components reside. The test/ folder is where you would provide any tests for your components. The rest is pretty much standard.

A typical workflow is to have a separate project where you test your components in an existing application as a feature. This will allow you to rapidly correct any issues and then transfer any changes to this project. You will need to save your changes to your Git repository. Finally, you can publish your repository to the Node Package Manager with the following command:

Code Listing 134

```
npm publish ./
```

If you haven't already set up your **npm** author info, you will need to have following before you can publish:

Code Listing 135

```
npm set init.author.name "Your name"
npm set init.author.email "your@email.com"
npm set init.author.url "http://yourblog.com"


npm adduser
```

You will be able to make changes to your Git repository and commit, but you will need to update the version in your package.json file before you try and publish again, as it will complain that you already have that version published.

The last step would be to consume the plugin from another project. You will first want to install the plugin using the following command:

Code Listing 136

```
npm install --save aurelia-succinctly
```

Finally, you will want to be sure that your main.js file includes the plugin as follows:

Code Listing 137

```
import '../styles/styles.css';
import 'font-awesome/css/font-awesome.css';
import 'bootstrap/dist/css/bootstrap.css';
import 'bootstrap';


import * as Bluebird from 'bluebird';
Bluebird.config({ warnings: false });


export async function configure(aurelia) {
 aurelia.use
  .standardConfiguration()
```

```
  .developmentLogging()
  .plugin('aurelia-succinctly');


  await aurelia.start();
  aurelia.setRoot('app');
}
```

This is a lot more complicated than just working with a feature, but once you have all the pieces in place, third-party developers will simply be able to install your plugin and update their main.js file, and they are ready to go.

Chapter 17 Testing

Overview

Testing is an important part of the development process, and Aurelia fully embraces support for testing your code as well as its core components. The Skeleton Navigation project has some good examples of unit tests and end-to-end tests, and we will be following the way they have testing set up.

File structure

The following is the way the skeleton navigation has its file structure for testing:

Code Listing 138

```
skeleton-esnext-webpack/
 node_modules/
 src/
 my-element.html
 my-element.js
 ...
 test/
 e2e/
  demo.spec.js
  skeleton.po.js
  ...
 unit/
  my-element.spec.js
  setup.js
  ...
 index.html
 ...
```

We have removed a lot of files to keep things simple. As you add screens or custom elements to your source, you should also add a corresponding unit and end-to-end test as necessary.

Unit tests

We should be able to test all of our views and view-models regardless of whether they are screens or custom elements. Let's define a simple custom element and see what it takes to test it. First, consider the my-element.html file:

Code Listing 139

```
<template>
  <div class="username">${username}</div>
</template>
```

Next, let's look at my-element.js to see the view-model:

Code Listing 140

```
import {customElement, bindable} from 'aurelia-framework';


@customElement('my-element')
export class MyElement {
  @bindable username = '';
}
```

Now, let's look at how we would test this element:

Code Listing 141

```
import {MyElement} from '../../src/my-element';


describe('the MyElement component', () => {
  var sut;


  beforeEach(() => {
  sut = new MyElement();
  });


  it('default username value', () => {
  expect(sut.username).toEqual('');
  });
});
```

As your views or custom elements get more complex, so will your tests.

 Note: Aurelia also has the ability to test custom elements and custom attributes in a mini Aurelia application, but at the time of writing this, there is a bug with the WebPack version. The Aurelia team is working hard on getting this fixed.

Please refer to the following link to see more on testing.

End-to-end tests

End-to-end tests allow you to load and interact with pages and assert the results. End-to-end tests will always start with the demo.spec.js file. It is this file that will reference all other pages, referred to as page objects. The page objects are helper files per page that facilitate manipulating the page. Your tests will reside inside the demo.spec.js file, and you will evaluate your tests there.

The following is an example of the welcome.po.js file:

Code Listing 142

```
export class PageObjectWelcome {


  constructor() {


  }


  getGreeting() {
  return element(by.tagName('h2')).getText();
  }


  setFirstname(value) {
  return element(by.valueBind('firstName')).clear().sendKeys(value);
  }


  setLastname(value) {
  return element(by.valueBind('lastName')).clear().sendKeys(value);
  }


  getFullname() {
  return element(by.css('.help-block')).getText();
  }


  pressSubmitButton() {
  return element(by.css('button[type="submit"]')).click();
```

```
  }


  openAlertDialog() {

  return browser.wait(() => {

    this.pressSubmitButton();


    return browser.wait(ExpectedConditions.alertIsPresent(), 5000).th
en(

      browser.switchTo().alert().then(

        // use alert.accept instead of alert.dismiss which results in a
browser crash

        function(alert) { alert.accept(); return true; },

        function() { return false; }

      )

    );

  });

  }

}
```

Let's now look at the demo.spec.js file and see how this file is used:

Code Listing 143

```
import {PageObjectWelcome} from './welcome.po.js';

import {PageObjectSkeleton} from './skeleton.po.js';


describe('aurelia skeleton app', function() {

  let poWelcome;

  let poSkeleton;


  beforeEach(() => {

  poSkeleton = new PageObjectSkeleton();

  poWelcome = new PageObjectWelcome();


  browser.loadAndWaitForAureliaPage('http://localhost:19876');
```

```
  });


  it('should load the page and display the initial page title', () =
> {
  expect(poSkeleton.getCurrentPageTitle()).toBe('Welcome | Aurelia')
;
  });


  it('should display greeting', () => {
  expect(poWelcome.getGreeting()).toBe('Welcome to the Aurelia Navig
ation App!');
  });


  it('should automatically write down the fullname', () => {
  poWelcome.setFirstname('Rob');
  poWelcome.setLastname('Eisenberg');

  // For now there is a timing issue with the binding.
  // Until resolved we will use a short sleep to overcome the issue.
  browser.sleep(200);
  expect(poWelcome.getFullname()).toBe('ROB EISENBERG');
  });


  it('should show alert message when clicking submit button', () =>
{
  expect(poWelcome.openAlertDialog()).toBe(true);
  });


  it('should navigate to users page', () => {
  poSkeleton.navigateTo('#/users');
  expect(poSkeleton.getCurrentPageTitle()).toBe('Github Users | Aure
lia');
  });
});
```

As you can see, we are importing our page object files and initializing them for testing. Take care to note that we use the `browser.sleep` function in order to interrogate the values from the pages after we have updated certain elements. Without this, we would evaluate too soon.

View-spy and compile-spy

Most web developers use the debugger right in their favorite browsers to step through their code and make sense of any issues they may have. Aurelia has two special templating behaviors that can really help:

- `view-spy`–Provides a copy of the `view` object into the console.
- `compile-spy`–Emits the compiler's `TargetInstruction`.

You need to be sure you have the `aurelia-testing` module installed. You can do this by executing the following:

Code Listing 144

```
npm install --save-dev aurelia-testing
```

Let's take a look at the welcome.html file from the Skeleton Navigation project:

Code Listing 145

```html
<template>
  <require from="aurelia-testing/view-spy"></require>
  <require from="aurelia-testing/compile-spy"></require>


  <section class="au-animate" view-spy compile-spy>
  <h2>${heading}</h2>
  <form role="form" submit.delegate="submit()">
    <div class="form-group">
    <label for="fn">First Name</label>
    <input type="text" value.bind="firstName" class="form-control" id
="fn" placeholder="first name">
    </div>
    <div class="form-group">
    <label for="ln">Last Name</label>
    <input type="text" value.bind="lastName" class="form-control" id=
"ln" placeholder="last name">
    </div>
    <div class="form-group">
    <label>Full Name</label>
    <p class="help-block">${fullName | upper}</p>
```

```
    </div>

    <button type="submit" class="btn btn-default">Submit</button>

    </form>

    </section>

</template>
```

We introduced the `require` tags to bring in the `view-spy` and `compile-spy`, respectively. Next, we added these custom attributes to the `section` tag. Let's take a look at what we would see in the browser:

Figure 35: View-Spy and Compile-Spy

Once you learn this trick, you will find it a great debugging tool to further help you with your mastery of Aurelia.

Chapter 18 Bundling

As you reach a critical point in your application, you will want to be able to bundle it for deployment. It is possible to do this using a variety of ways, but we will look at doing this using WebPack. The command is simple: simply type the following into your console:

Code Listing 146

```
npm run build
```

This will create a development bundle and place it into the dist/ folder.

If you wish to have your bundle optimized and minified for production, you can enter the following command:

Code Listing 147

```
npm run build:prod
```

To test either a development build or a production build, enter the following command:

Code Listing 148

```
npm run server:prod
```

You should get something similar to the following output:

Figure 36: Running a development or production bundle.

Then, if you navigate to http://192.168.1.9:8080, you should see the same output as before (when you were developing).

> *Note: If you wish to target production in your bundle, be sure to set your NODE_ENV variable to production so that the webpack-dev-server.js does not load into the browser.*

Don't forget that you can always go back to your development workflow and have your changes update your browser automatically by going back to the following command:

Code Listing 149

```
npm start
```
This should at least get you started in the right direction when it comes to bundling.

Chapter 19 Deploying

In this chapter, I am going to walk you through taking your application and bundling it, then deploying it to GitHub or Bitbucket pages so that you can see it running. The steps required to do this will not be exactly the same as you would do for production on one of your own servers, but it should be close enough to give you a starting point.

The steps that we are going to follow should work for both GitHub and Bitbucket repositories. Before we start, it is recommended that you have two repositories: one repository that stores your source code for development, and another repository that only contains your bundle for deployment. The following steps assume that you already have a development repository set up. Let's get started:

1. Create a user account on GitHub or Bitbucket, if you don't already have one.
2. Create a deployment project.
3. Clone this new project to your development machine.
4. In your existing project on your development machine, execute: `npm run build`
5. From the dist/ folder, copy its contents to the new project: `cp ../<project name>/*`
6. In your terminal window in the new project, add the files using Git.
7. Commit your changes to the new project.
8. Push your changes to GitHub or Bitbucket.
9. Test your application by navigating to:
   a. For Bitbucket: http://<user account>.bitbucket.org
   b. For GitHub: http://<user account>.github.io

This will come in handy when you are simply trying to test your application and you want it pushed somewhere easy and free, but without a lot of ceremony.

Here are links to GitHub and Bitbucket in case you run into any issues.

Remember, you can only have one set of pages per user account. Also, this only works if your code is front-end only. If your project has both client and server mixed together, then you may need to do some additional work.

Deployment security

We have been focusing on building applications using Aurelia. At some point, you will be deploying your solution to the web, and end users will view the application through their browsers. It is important keep your source code secure and try to mitigate third parties from copying your source code and throwing up their own solution. Here are a few points to take into consideration when deploying your solution:

- Never deploy your source files. Always bundle your application.
- Even if you bundle your source files, always ensure you have minified your bundle as well.
- If you want to further obfuscate your source, consider looking at jscrambler.
- Aurelia has working server-side delivery of pages and content; consider using this technology, and only load content as you need it.
- If you are using third-party services or tools, never store your user accounts, IDs, or passwords in your source code.
- Consider configuring your server to host your application using HTTPS.
- If you are enabling CORS on your server, do not configure with wild cards for any access.

Chapter 20 Closing Thoughts

Step back and give yourself a pat on the back for completing this introduction to Aurelia. Learning new frameworks is time consuming and requires a lot of effort and dedication on your part. Aurelia is one of the easiest frameworks to learn, as it tries to stay consistent with standards around JavaScript and HTML. With the knowledge you learned from this book, you should now be able to build really awesome web applications. Remember that there are a lot of paths to getting started. Whether it is from the navigation skeleton samples or using the Aurelia CLI, you will be able to get yourself up and running very quickly. Don't forget to use Gitter and StackOverflow as resources to help you when you have questions. Finally, there are so many plugins for Aurelia that make your development workflow easier. Whatever you do, don't give up, you have already completed the hard part by learning the framework! Now get out there and build an awesome web application!

Again, thanks for reading the book and best of luck with your development!

www.ingramcontent.com/pod-product-compliance
Lightning Source LLC
Chambersburg PA
CBHW071003050326
40689CB00014B/3478